Welcome to Mexico

Mona King

Collins
Glasgow and London

Cover Photographs
Van Phillips: Acapulco Bay; one of the Atlantes at Tula;
the Flower Gardens of Xochimilco

Marcos Ortiz: Feather Dancer, Oaxaca;
Chloe Sayer: Mexican girl at Chichén Itzá

Publicite Gerard (A. G. Fromenti): chac-mool at Cancún

Photographs
J. Allan Cash Ltd
pp. 55, 74, 87, 99, 100, 102, 106

The Photo Source
pp. 35, 81, 82 (col 2)

Van Phillips
pp. 43 (col 2), 46, 69 (col 2), 73, 96, 119

Picturepoint
pp. 40, 52 (col 1), 53, 57, 58, 60, 61, 62, 66, 69 (top), 70,
71, 72, 77, 82 (col 1), 83, 88, 90 (col 2), 93,
94, 95, 107, 115, 124

Popperfoto
27, 120, 123

Publicite Gerard (A. G. Fromenti)
pp. 52 (col 2), 67, 111, 114, 116

Marcos Ortiz
pp. 49, 84, 125 (Chloe Sayer: pp. 69, col 1)

Topham
p.23

ZEFA
pp. 43 (col 1), 43 (bottom), 90 (col 1)

Regional maps and map of Ancient Mexico (pp. 32, 33)
Mike Shand

Town Plans
M. and R. Piggott

Ground Plans
devized and drawn by M. and R. Piggott based on material
in the following publications: Monuments of Civilization Maya,
Cassell (1975); The Ancient Kingdoms of Mexico, Allen Lane (1982);
The Aztecs, Maya and their Predecessors, Academic Press (1981);
Tula, Thames and Hudson (1983)

Illustration
pp. 6-7 Peter Joyce

First published 1986
Copyright © text: Mona King 1986
Copyright © maps: Wm. Collins Sons & Co. Ltd.
Published by William Collins Sons and Company Limited
Printed in Great Britain
ISBN 0 00 447372 8

HOW TO USE THIS BOOK

The contents page of this book is divided up into tourist regions.
The book is in two main sections: general information and gazetteer.
In the gazetteer each tourist region has an introduction and a
regional map (detail below left).
There are also town plans of Mexico City and Guadalajara (detail below right).
All main entries listed in the gazetteer are shown in the regional maps.
Places to visit and leisure facilities available in each region and city are indicated by symbols.
Main roads, railways and airports are shown on the maps.

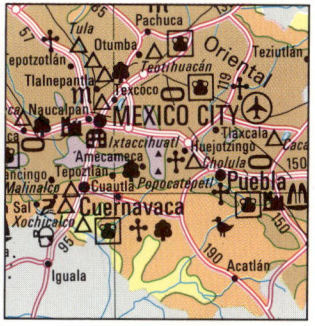

Regional Maps

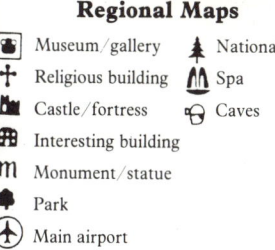

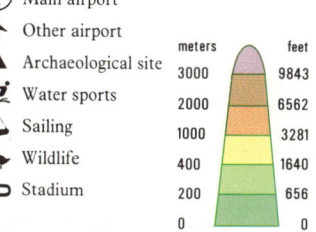

Town Plans

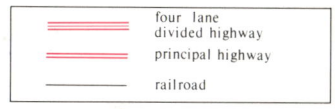

Every effort has been made to give you an up-to-date text but changes are constantly occurring and we will be grateful for any information about changes you may notice while traveling.

6 The Northwest
19 Sonora
20 Sinaloa
21 Nayarit

5 Baja California
17 Baja California Norte
18 Baja California Sur

3 The West
7 Jalisco
8 Colima
9 Michoacán

CONTENTS

Mexico	6
History	8
The Arts	10
Paperwork	12
Customs	13
Currency	13
How to Get There	14
Internal Travel	15
If You are Driving	17
Where to Stay	18
Food and Drink	20
Enjoy Yourself	22
Entertainment	25
Fiestas	26
What You Need to Know	28
Useful Addresses	31
The Language	31
Ancient Mexico	32
The South	49
The Yucatán Peninsula	63
The West	75
Central Mexico	85
Baja California	97
The Northwest	103
The North	109
The Northeast	113

The Gulf Region	117
Town Plans	
1. Mexico City	36-40
2. Guadalajara	78-79
Ground Plans	
1. Monte Albán	56
2. Palenque	58
3. Chichén Itzá	68
4. Uxmal	73
5. Teotihuacán	92

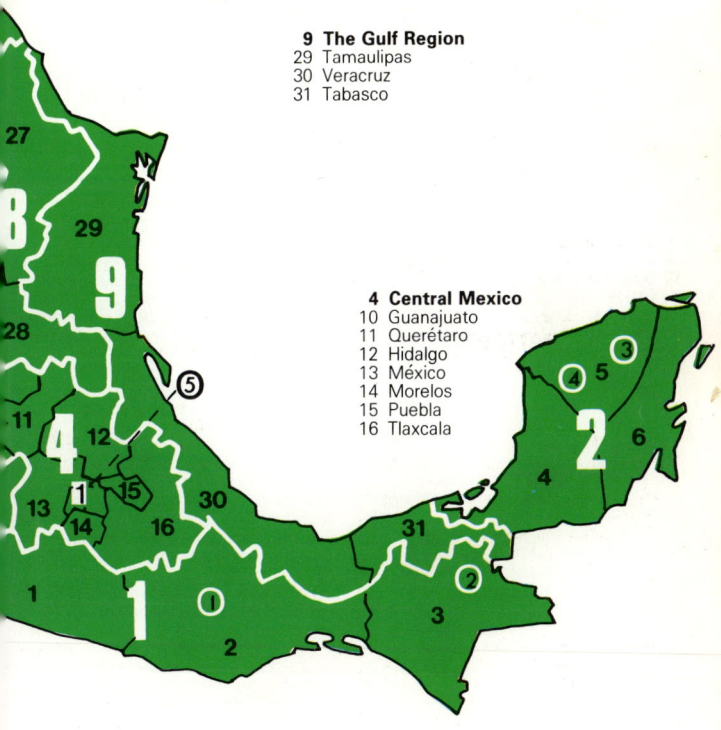

7 The North
22 Chihuahua
23 Coahuila
24 Durango
25 Zacatecas
26 Aguascalientes

8 The Northeast
27 Nuevo León
28 San Luis Potosí

9 The Gulf Region
29 Tamaulipas
30 Veracruz
31 Tabasco

4 Central Mexico
10 Guanajuato
11 Querétaro
12 Hidalgo
13 México
14 Morelos
15 Puebla
16 Tlaxcala

1 The South
1 Guerrero
2 Oaxaca
3 Chiapas

2 The Yucatán Peninsula
4 Campeche
5 Yucatán
6 Quintana Roo

MEXICO

Mexico is a land of colorful contrast. On a journey through the country, visitors are struck by the remarkable range of cultures, geography and climate. Mexico City, with its huge population, is one of the liveliest cities in the world but you do not have to travel far to visit some charming little Indian villages. Archaeological sites, dating back to the times of the Maya and the Aztecs, abound and there are many towns which display attractive examples of Spanish colonial architecture. The scenery is often breathtaking and the magnificent mountain ranges serve as a picturesque backdrop to many towns and cities.

Mexico is the third largest nation in Latin America and is about one fourth the size of the United States. The east coast (on the Gulf of Mexico and the Caribbean) and the west coast (on the Pacific Ocean) provide excellent beaches. To the north, Mexico shares a 2000 mile (3200 km) boundary with the United States and, to the south, it is bordered by Guatemala and Belize. The population is currently estimated at 78 million and is rapidly increasing. More than half of Mexico's citizens are under 20 years of age.

This is a country of dramatic and varied landscapes: towering mountains, and broad plateaux, mighty canyons and plunging gorges; vast expanses of arid desert in the north are replaced by fresh, alpine forests of the central regions and the lush, tropical jungles of the south. Two great mountain ranges, the Sierra Madre Occidental and the Sierra Madre Oriental, sweep down the west and east of the country from the United States border. The central elevated plateau is dominated by lofty mountains, many of volcanic origin. This region is considered the historic heart of Mexico and most of its major cities, including the capital, Mexico City, are located here. The tall, snow-covered volcanoes which dominate this area are a beautiful feature of Mexico and form a geographical division between north and south. Tallest peaks are *Pico de Orizaba* or 'Morning Star' which, at a height of 18,700 ft (5700 m), is the highest in Mexico; *Popocatépetl,* known as the Smoking Mountain; *Ixtaccíhuatl,* known as 'the Sleeping Woman' and *Nevado de Toluca.* There are numerous lakes and lagoons to explore. The largest is Lake Chapala, situated in the west of Mexico, near Guadalajara. There are only a few rivers and they are not usually navigable.

Temperatures and rainfall vary so

greatly in Mexico because they are influenced by altitudes and the relationship to coasts and mountain ranges. There are three main climatic zones: the *tierras calientes,* or hot lands; *tierras templadas,* temperate areas; *tierras frías,* cold lands. The hot lands stretch along southern tropical coastlines, up to an altitude of about 3000 ft (900 m). The temperate zone which can be found at an altitude above this up to 6000 ft, enjoys a pleasing, spring-like climate throughout the year. The cold lands are above 6000 ft, with fairly warm days and cool to cold nights. With the exception of the dry desert plains in the north, where rainfall is minimal, the rainy season in Mexico lasts from late May to October. You can expect rainfall to be most frequent in the southern jungles. As Mexico lies in the Northern Hemisphere, with the tropic of Cancer running through the central part, its summer months coincide with those in the United States and Europe. May is usually particularly hot during the summer but the winter months, when the weather is pleasant, are ideal for visitors.

Mexico has a rich flora and fauna. There are thousands of varieties of plants and flowers to view in the countryside including many different types of orchid. The Mexican landscape is well-known for its cacti and there are more species of cactus to be found here than in any other country in the world. Hundreds of different birds make their home here and there are several varieties of humming bird. Hunting is a popular sport in Mexico where there are many wild animals but in National Parks the animals are protected. Mexico's waters in the Pacific, the Gulf of Mexico and the Caribbean are ideal for fishermen. The waters abound with many varieties of fish.

The Spanish conquest of Mexico in 1521 resulted in the merging of two great cultures — Mexican Indian and Hispanic. The race which has evolved from this are today's Mexicans, descended from Indian and Spanish ancestors and they are known

as *mestizos*. There is a small minority of people who were born in Mexico but have pure Spanish blood. These people are known as *creoles*. Mexican Indians who have no Spanish blood and speak in their native tongue, are estimated to make up about 13% of the population.

The Mexican can be a complex character, with many different facets to his nature. He is generally proud of his heritage and can show a quiet stoicism and dignity — a common Indian trait. He can also be completely spontaneous and display a warmth and generosity more characteristic of his Spanish forefathers.

Courtesy and good manners are observed by all Mexicans. They are often very sensitive and can have their pride hurt easily by a misdirected joke or comment but compliments and courteous treatment on the part of the visitor are always greeted warmly. The Mexican is known for his generous hospitality and the expression in Spanish *'Mi casa es su casa'*, which means 'my house is your house' is commonly used. Family ties are very strong and members are extremely protective toward each other.

The Mexican has a unique love of humanity and will go to great lengths to be helpful. The mañana image is a popular one and is well-described by the lighthearted saying, 'never do today what you can put off until tomorrow and never do yourself tomorrow what you can get someone else to do for you!' Most Mexicans have little regard for the clock. If you arrange to meet a Mexican, do not expect him to turn up on time. In fact, he may not arrive at all! There is another type of Mexican who is dynamic, go-ahead and works amazingly long hours but he still finds the time for leisure. Even when things seem to be at their lowest ebb, the Mexican will still go out to eat and enjoy himself, shrugging off tomorrow's problems. Most Mexicans have a wonderful sense of humor and delight in jokes of all sorts.

Vast new oil fields discovered in recent years around the Gulf of Mexico have provided Mexico with its number one industry. Mexico has become one of the largest oil producing nations in the world. Mining has been a major industry since colonial times and there are good supplies of valuable materials for excavation, including silver and some gold.

Agriculture is very important to Mexico and technical aid in recent times has enabled farmers to grow a variety of important crops, with a surplus for export. Major products include coffee, cotton, sugar, beans, maize, alfalfa, rice, tobacco, citrus and tropical fruits. Large irrigation projects in arid areas have greatly increased the availability of arable land.

Traditional crafts are still practiced today, and an enormous amount of hand-blown glassware, ceramics, artifacts of onyx, woven materials and other attractive arts and crafts are produced.

Tourism is very important to Mexico's economy and is second only to the oil industry as the biggest earner of foreign exchange. Miguel Alemán, President of Mexico from 1946 to 1952, saw the potential of the little fishing village of Acapulco and initiated its development in the mid-1950's. As President of the Mexican National Tourist Council, he made a tremendous contribution towards the promotion of tourism in Mexico. There are now numerous popular resorts along the Pacific and Caribbean coasts, with magnificent hotels and excellent facilities. The Government agency FONATUR, was set up about 10 years ago to develop new areas of tourism and to provide employment for Mexicans. Cancun, on the Caribbean coast, and Ixtapa, on the Pacific, are its main success stories and there are more projects underway in other areas.

The official name of Mexico, which is a Federal Republic, is 'Los estados unidos Mexicanos' (United Mexican states). There are 31 states and a Federal District in which the Capital city and seat of government is situated. The 1917 constitution is the law of the land and it vests legislative power in the National Congress. This consists of a Senate and a Chamber of Deputies. Senators serve a six-year term. Of the Deputies, 300 are elected by majority vote and up to 100 are elected by proportional representation. All deputies serve a three-year term. The President, whose influence and word is very important, serves a six-year term and he is not allowed to seek re-election. Each state has its own constitution, handled by a Chamber of Deputies and a Governor, also elected for six years.

Our gazetteer section covers all 31 states and the Federal District. They are divided into ten tourist sections, the boundaries of which have been determined by geographical and political borders, taking tourist interest into account: The **South,** including Acapulco — the scenic areas of Guerrero, Oaxaca and Chiapas; the **Yucatán Peninsula** — charming resorts and fascinating ancient ruins; the **West** is possibly the most scenic part of Mexico; **Central Mexico** encircles Mexico City and is the liveliest, richest area of the country; hunting, fishing, bird-watching, fossil collecting and surfing are big attractions in **Baja California;** the **Northwest** is known for its beautiful coastline; the **North** is famous for its spectacular Copper Canyon; the mountain ranges and magnificent views of the **Northeast;** the **Gulf Region** is of great historical interest; **Mexico City** — an exciting city with a history dating back to the Aztec's first arrival in the Valley of Mexico.

HISTORY

Little is known of Mexico's very earliest civilizations. Popular theory suggests that nomadic tribes crossed the Bering Straits from Asia during the Ice Age, when the continents were still connected, and they are thought to have arrived in Mexico about 20,000 years ago. Many Mexicans today still show traces of the Oriental features of their remote ancestors.

The Olmec culture was the first highly developed civilization to flourish in Mesoamerica — around the year 1000 BC in the coastal regions around Veracruz and Tabasco. They produced sculptures of gigantic proportions with colossal heads and negroid features. They were also skilled potters and were able to develop a good understanding of mathematics, devizing a calendar system.

Other tribes which followed were clearly influenced by the Olmecs. Among the most significant civilizations which began to develop subsequently were the Teotihuacános in the Valley of Mexico, the Zapotecs around Oaxaca, and the Maya in the southeast. Teotihuacán was probably the first real city to be established in the Valley. It is thought to have been constructed around 300 BC and was inhabited by a tribe which we call Teotihuacános, but their true origins and identity have never been established. They remained there until about AD 700 and their influence was far reaching. Irrigation in the area supported a large population. The mighty Pyramid of the Sun and Pyramid of the Moon are among the many impressive pyramids and temples which remain as relics of this once powerful city. Around AD 700 Teotihuacán's reign came to an end when northerners began settling around the shores of the lakes in central Mexico.

The Zapotec civilization is believed to have descended directly from the Olmecs. They dominated the Valley of Oaxaca and developed the magnificent city of Monte Albán, which was later taken over by the Mixtecs from further north, who turned it from a Holy City into a regal cemetery. Mitla, in the vicinity, is another important center which is believed to have been originated by the Zapotecs but which bears strong evidence of Mixtec influence.

Perhaps the greatest of the pre-Columbian civilizations was that of the Maya who were probably also descended from the Olmecs. The first traces of civilization were found in Guatemala. They gradually migrated northward to the Yucatán Peninsula and by about AD 200 they were building temples and pyramids and their empire extended over a vast area of southeast Mexico and parts of Central America. They were skilled mathematicians and architects and had made astonishing astronomical calculations, devizing a most accurate calendar.

This highly advanced culture began to decline around the 10th century and it was also about this time that the warlike Toltecs from their capital, Tula, in the Valley of Mexico took over sites in the Yucatán Peninsula. Here they exercised their influence over the Maya, introducing new cultures and bringing new skills. They built over and around existing Mayan cities, of which a classic example is Chichén Itzá. The Mayan and Toltec culture declined for unknown reasons about a century before the Spaniards arrived in the mid-16th century and cities were abandoned to the jungle. Other important centers include El Tajín, city of the Totonacs in the state of Veracruz, and deserted around AD 1100; Cholula, near Puebla, to the southeast of Mexico City, where you can visit the pyramid (which covers the largest area in the world) called Tepanapa.

Around the middle of the thirteenth century, the Aztecs, who were the last and most famous of Mexico's nomadic tribes, arrived in the Valley of Mexico. The sight of an eagle perched on a cactus devouring a snake was, they believed, the fulfillment of a prophecy and a sign that this spot, on an island in the middle of Lake Texcoco, was to be the site of their capital city, Tenochtitlán. The symbol of the eagle, cactus and snake now appears on Mexico's flag.

The Aztecs were fierce and aggressive, swiftly conquering neighboring tribes and establishing an empire of far-reaching influence. Led by their god of war, Huitzilopochtli, they practiced human sacrificial rites. They were ingenious engineers and the city they built on the lake with causeways connecting it to the mainland was quite a feat of skillful engineering. By the mid-16th century, they were the richest and most powerful tribe in Mexico.

Spaniard, Hernández de Córdoba discovered the Yucatán Peninsula in 1517. The following year, Juan Grijalva landed on the island of Cozumel in the Caribbean, passing the large and impressive clifftop city of Tulum on the way. In 1519 Hernán Cortés set out from Cuba with 550 men and horses and landed near Veracruz. Burning his boats so that his men could not turn back, he and his followers set forth on their expedition to the Aztec capital, receiving support en route from the Totonac Indians and later the Tlaxcalans who were bitterly opposed to the Aztecs. The Aztecs had never seen horses before or men of Spanish skin coloring. After two years of bitter fighting Cortés and his army of Spaniards and Indians conquered Tenochtitlán. The Aztec empire was finished. A new era began in the history of Mexico, with the birth of a new nation of Hispanic cultures exerting their influence and merging with old Indian customs and traditions. The Spanish immediately began constructing a new capital on the ruins of the old Aztec site and Mexico City was born. The country was divided into huge estates under Spanish landlords. Cortés was named Governor of New Spain, as it was called and in 1528 he returned to Spain for two years. The first Viceroy of New Spain, Don Antonio de Mendoza, arrived in 1535 and throughout the 300 years of colonial rule, the country was governed by a succession of Viceroys. The Spanish developed the natural resources of the country, in particular the gold and silver mining industries, and they built many beautiful cities with palacial mansions and exquisite churches. Ironically, the upheavals of the early part of the 19th century which finally led to the War of Independence, were largely caused by the increasing number of Spaniards born in Mexico. On the night of September 15th, 1810, Father Hidalgo, the parish priest at the village of Dolores in Guanajuato state, rang the church bell signalling the start of the struggle for Independence against the Spanish. After years of fighting and battles, Independence was gained in 1822 and the new republic came into existence. The last Spanish Viceroy returned to Spain and Augustín de Iturbide proclaimed himself Emperor of Mexico. The years following Independence were very unsettled and in less than a year General Santa Ana had taken over in a military coup. In 1829 Spanish forces made an unsuccessful attempt to recover Mexico and in 1836 fighting broke out between the United States and Mexico. That same year Santa Ana defeated Texan forces at the Alamo but he was overcome soon after by Sam Houston's American forces at San Jacinto and Texas was separated from Mexico. In 1846 the United States declared war on Mexico and invaded. That year, under the leadership of Santa Ana, Mexico ceded about half its territory including California, Arizona and New Mexico to the United States for a sum of money.

The country's troubles continued and in 1861, following further conflict, Benito Juárez took over the bankrupt country and suspended payment of foreign debts. The following year, allied forces of France, Spain and Great Britain, to whom substantial sums were owed, landed at Veracruz to ensure payment of the debts but when France's intention to claim sovereignty became clear, the Spanish and British withdrew. In 1864, the ill-fated Archduke Maximilian, who was the brother of Hapsburg Emperor Franz Josef, arrived in Mexico with his wife Carlota and was installed by the French as Emperor of Mexico. In 1867 French troops, who had been occupying the country were recalled by Napoléon III, leaving Maximilian completely vulnerable. Juárez, who had been exiled, rallied an army and marched against him. Maximilian was defeated by Juárez' army in Querétaro and executed on the Hill of Bells, above the town. Juárez then resumed his position as President until his death in 1872.

The Juárez Law was drafted during his term, improving human rights and bringing agricultural reform while the privileges of the Catholic Church and those of the military were attacked. This dark, brooding Indian from the area of Oaxaca was a liberal who showed great concern for the people of the nation and is regarded as one of Mexico's greatest heroes. Lerdo de Tejada, who took over, was unpopular and in 1876 General Porfirio Díaz was elected as President. During the period of his Presidency until 1910, railways were built, oil discoveries were made and industry and foreign investment were developed. Díaz laid the foundations of modern, industrialized Mexico. Unfortunately, he neglected the agricultural problems and land ownership was the main cause of the Revolution of 1910, led by Francisco Madero. Díaz was defeated and went into exile. In 1911, Madero was installed as President but he was assassinated two years later and there followed ten years of turbulence and bitter fighting, with the emergence of such prominent figures and heroes of the Revolution as Emiliano Zapata and the flamboyant Pancho Villa. In 1917 a new constitution was drawn up in Querétaro and this still serves today. After the Revolution, reconstruction gradually began and order was restored. In 1934 the Party of Revolutionary Institution, or PRI, as it is called, was formed and is still the predominant political party. Lázaro Cárdenas, who was elected as President in 1934 carried out large scale land reforms and in 1938 expropriated the oil and nationalized the industry. He was considered one of Mexico's great Presidents.

Mexico today has governmental stability and there are modern schools, hospitals and programs for public works. Politically it is a democracy, but there is only one ruling party, the PRI which has no significant opposition. The discovery of huge oil deposits around the gulf regions created an industrial boom. Later as world prices decreased in 1982, Mexico encountered an economic crisis as interest rates fell and Mexico's foreign debts rose steeply. President de la Madrid, who took office in 1982, inherited this serious situation and had to introduce cuts in public spending. In September 1985, Mexico City and surrounding states suffered a series of tragic and damaging earthquakes. At the time of writing, the extent of the disaster in loss of lives, property and income can only be estimated but it is already clear that the Mexicans desire to help one another in times of adversity will enable them to get their cities back to normal and will ensure that the social and political foundations, which have been Mexico's strength in recent times, remain unharmed.

THE ARTS

Early Civilizations

There are still numerous examples of art produced in Mexico before the Spanish conquest in 1521. The earliest artists were able to express themselves in many forms. Today visitors and historians alike discover that it gives a fascinating insight into the customs and traditions of the many tribes and groups who inhabited the country in ancient times.

The mysterious Olmecs from the Gulf region dominated art between 1500 BC and 300 BC. They were the first Mesoamerican people to construct pyramid bases for temples. They worked precious stones and carved sculptures and giant monolithic heads with negroid features. Other civilizations of the period produced mainly pottery. Pottery produced in the western coastal regions of Colima and Nayarit was more highly developed. During the 'classic' era, between 300 BC and AD 900, great cities were constructed and it was a period of fine architectural achievement. Magnificent pyramids with stucco reliefs, murals and carved heads of gods and animals, can be found in Teotihuacán, the first proper city in Mesoamerica. The Zapotecs, who dominated the Valley of Oaxaca built Monte Albán and their architecture shows Olmec influence. Large tombs, plazas and truncated pyramids were a feature. Archaeological sites from pre-Columbian Mexico are described more fully in the gazetteer. Maya culture spread over a large area which included southeast Mexico and much of Central America. They were the most advanced of the Mesoamerican civilizations and built numerous large ceremonial centers, the greatest of which are Palenque, Uxmal and Chichén Itzá (Mayan and Toltec). Classical Maya style is characterized by steep pyramids, low relief decoration on the walls and the Mayan arch. They produced 'codices' with hieroglyphic writing, most of which were destroyed by the Spaniards. The Maya were also skilled jade workers and decorated their pottery with stylized motifs. Mayan murals at Bonampak in Chiapas are considered to be great works of art. The Totonacs and Huastecs from the northerly regions of the Gulf of Mexico were skilled potters and constructed the outstanding Pyramid of the Niches at El Tajín.

Around 1000 AD, the Toltecs settled in the Valley of Mexico after the fall of the great classic civilizations and built their capital, Tula. Buildings were decorated with predominant themes of eagles, jaguars, warriors and plumed serpents symbolizing their deity, Quetzalcóatl, known as the Plumed Serpent.

They also sculpted *chac-mools* — reclining figures with a receptacle for living hearts, which were used during sacrificial rites.

The Mixtecs, who took over the Oaxaca area from the Zapotecs, produced fine pottery, metalwork and hieroglyphic scroll paintings. They were renowned for their geometric decorations on buildings, made from thousands of small carved stones.

The Aztecs, who inhabited the Valley of Mexico from the mid-14th century until the destruction of their civilization by the Spaniards in the mid-16th century, built large palaces and steep pyramids which bear some resemblance to earlier Mayan architecture. Their sculptures depicted gods and images of gruesome scenes, and human sacrifices were very much in evidence. Recent excavations at the Aztec Templo Mayor in Mexico City have revealed fine examples of jewelry, pottery and engravings from this era.

Post-conquest

Painting: during the colonial era, which began in the middle of the 16th century, most paintings related to religion and many of the best during this period can be found in churches and cathedrals. After the turmoils of the 1910-1920 Revolution, a new cultural product was born in the form of the muralist movement. The tradition of decorating buildings, which continued from pre-Hispanic times through the colonial period, had disappeared after Independence from Spain in 1821. This was revived by the Revolution when governments started commissioning murals for public buildings in an attempt to encourage a new sense of national identity and an appreciation of Mexico's Indian heritage. Today these murals are considered Mexico's most distinctive form of painting. The most important muralists were Diego Rivera, José Clemente Orozco and David Alfaro Siqueiros. Perhaps the greatest was Diego Rivera. He had a flamboyant character and a wonderful sense of color. His murals depicted significant events in the history of Mexico, blending pagan and Christian themes. Among his most striking murals are those adorning the main stairway at the Palacio Nacional in Mexico City.

Orozco was an idealist with a sense of tragedy and full of passion. You can visit some of Orozco's murals at the Hospicio Cabañas and the Palacio de Gobierno in Guadalajara, the town where he produced much of his work. Siqueiros was a political activist and his murals are bold and violent with colossal figures. One of his most famous murals, The March of Humanity, is at the Siqueiros Polyforum in Mexico City. At the University City in Mexico City, there are some excellent Siqueiros murals in the Rectory and the library building is famed for its exterior by Juan O'Gorman which is entirely covered by mosaics. Also in Mexico City, you can visit the Rufino Tamayo museum which contains many of this excellent 20th-century painter's works.

Architecture: following the Spanish conquest of Mexico in 1521, a new cultural era began. The architectural influence imposed by the Spaniards is visible even today. For 300 years, the Spaniards founded new towns and built churches and mansions. Architects were clearly influenced by European, and particularly Spanish architecture. Numerous monasteries and churches were built by friars of the Augustinian, Dominican, Franciscan and Jesuit orders. In those early years following the conquest, the Spaniards were well aware of the need for defense and many of their monasteries were constructed with this in mind. In the early 1600s the relationship between Spaniards and Indians began to be more relaxed and architects were able to take a greater interest in aesthetics. They began building in the Baroque style using ornamentation. One of the best examples of this can be found in the Santo Domingo church in Oaxaca.

As the Indians began to take an interest in architecture, their tendency to use excessive ornamentation began to appear in the design of some churches such as the Cathedral of Santiago in Saltillo. This Churrigueresque style can be described as an extreme overcrowding of decoration on all surfaces. More tasteful buildings in the Plateresque style were also constructed during the colonial period. This style is a combination of delicacy and restraint in ornamentation. The cathedral in Morelia is one of the finest examples of Plateresque architecture in Mexico with powerful, majestic towers which are well proportioned and delicately decorated.

Since the Revolution which ended in 1920, much of Mexico's architecture has been very modern and imaginative, such as the Chamber of Deputies in Campeche. Its shape has led locals to refer to it as the 'flying saucer'. Contemporary hotels at beach resorts are sometimes designed to resemble pyramids and temples of former times.

Literature: the printing press did not arrive in Mexico until 1536 and it was used mainly for documentation of Spanish achievements and exploration. Poetry was published but there were no novels. Juana Ines de la Cruz was an important poet of the 17th century and wrote many beautiful sonnets, lyrics and elegies.

The first newspaper was printed in 1784 and in the 1800s, the first novels began to appear. This was around the time of the Independence movement and most literature became a vehicle for political discussion but there were some notable novels: José Joaquin wrote *El Periquillo Sarnieto* in 1816 and it has been translated into English and published under the title *The Itching Parrot*. The works of Alfonso Reyes and Frederico Gamboa in the early 20th century are regarded very highly both in Mexico and abroad.

Today, novels and short stories by Carlo Fuentes are widely acclaimed. Mexico's leading dramatist is Rodolfo Usigli whose works include *Crown of Shadows* and *Crown of Light*.

PAPERWORK

U.S. citizens: if you are planning to visit Mexico you require either a single-entry or multiple-entry tourist card. Single-entry cards allow you to enter the country for a period normally up to 90 days. You can obtain one upon presentation of your passport, birth certificate, citizenship papers or voter's registration certificate as proof of United States citizenship. The single-entry card can be obtained from any Mexican Tourist Office, some travel agents, from airlines serving Mexico, a Mexican consulate or at the point of entry although this can cause border delays. Multiple-entry cards, which are issued usually for about 90 days, allow you to cross the border as often as you wish during the specified period. They can be obtained from a Mexican consulate upon showing proof of citizenship and three passport-size photographs are required. Tourist cards are issued free of charge. If you are visiting a border town for less than three days, you do not require a tourist card.

Children under 15 years of age may be included on a parent's card but it is better for each traveler to have his or her own separate card. A parent with a child listed on his or her card cannot leave Mexico without the child and in the event of illness or unforeseen circumstances this could present a problem. Persons under 18 years of age who plan to travel to Mexico without a parent or legal guardian must present to the Mexican consulate a notarized affidavit in duplicate signed by both parents or the legal guardian, granting permission to travel in Mexico. If traveling with one parent, there must be a notarized affidavit in duplicate signed by the parent who is remaining in the United States.

You can request a card before departure which allows you to stay for a maximum period of 180 days. Should you wish to extend your stay you should apply to Gobernación, Juárez 92, in Mexico City, or an office of the Immigration Department in one of the other major cities in the country. The top half of your tourist card serves as an entry permit and the copy must be given up at the border. When in Mexico, carry your card with you at all times and if you lose it, you should immediately report the loss to your nearest Mexican government tourist office which is authorized to replace it for you. No inoculations are necessary unless you have recently traveled to an infected area.

U.K. citizens: British subjects traveling to Mexico require a valid passport and a tourist card. The passport can be obtained from passport offices at the following addresses: Clive House, 70-78 Petty France, London SW1; India Buildings, Water St, Liverpool 2; Olympia House, Upper Dock St, Newport, Gwent; 55 Westfield Road, Peterborough; 1st floor, Empire House, West Nile St, Glasgow or enquire at main post offices. They can also be obtained in person only at Hampton House, 47-53 High St, Belfast and from Mexican consulates. Tourist cards are issued free (normally for a period of 90 days although a request can be made for 180 days) and no photographs are required. Applications can be made in person or in writing to the Mexican consulate (8 Halkin St, London SW1) enclosing your passport, or to the Mexican Tourist Office (7 Cork St, London W1), or authorized airlines, presenting, in each case, your passport which must be valid for at least 3 months. There are no health requirements.

Many air services from the United Kingdom to Mexico make a connection via the United States. To enter the United States, you should have a visa. Application can be made direct to the United States Embassy, Visa Branch, 5 Upper Grosvenor St, London W1 or through certain travel agents and United States carriers who can sometimes process this more rapidly. In any case, do allow plenty of time.

Canadian citizens: Canadians traveling to Mexico require a passport, a Canadian citizenship card or birth certificate and a tourist card. Passport applications may be made through post offices or passport offices throughout the country. Tourist cards are obtainable, free of charge from Mexican consulates in Montréal, Québec, Toronto or Vancouver, the Mexican Embassy in Ottawa, from offices of the Mexican Tourist office in Montréal, Toronto or Vancouver or from authorized airlines. There are no health requirements.

All visitors: you must enter Mexico within 90 days of the date of issue of your tourist card which otherwise becomes invalid. Remember to have your passport with you when changing travelers checks. People visiting Mexico on business or as students intending to study there should apply to their local Mexican consulate for information on requirements, photographs, procedures etc. although if your stay is to be relatively short, a tourist card may be sufficient.

Insurance: the visitor is strongly advised to take out insurance before departure. It is important to insure yourself against accidents or illness in Mexico. There are comprehensive short-term insurance policies which cover such events as loss of baggage and personal effects, accidents and sickness. These policies can be arranged through your travel agent or an insurance agent. Although loss or damage of luggage while traveling by air should be covered by the airline in question, protection offered is sometimes limited. Procedures can be lengthy and the end result is not always satisfactory. Any loss of baggage while traveling should be reported as soon as you arrive. You should also consider a policy which includes insurance against possible cancellation of your flight. In the event of cancellation due to sickness suffered by you or a close member of your family, you would be insured under this policy for a full refund of your fare. Some policies also cover flight insurance in case of injury on board. For information on car insurance, please see p. 17.

CUSTOMS

There are no restrictions on the amount of Mexican currency you arrive or leave with. When entering Mexico, you may bring the following items with you: Clothing and other articles for personal use; one still and one portable movie camera (8 mm or 16 mm) and up to 12 unexposed rolls of film; up to 20 books; fishing equipment, water skis, two tennis rackets or other portable sporting articles for personal use; up to 200 cigarettes, 50 cigars or 9 ounces (255 g) of tobacco; 3 U.S. quarts (3 liters) of alcohol; medicines: in the case of drugs a medical prescription is required; up to 6 gifts of a value not exceeding 5000 pesos; one portable TV set and one portable radio; one portable typewriter; one portable musical instrument; one tent and camping equipment; one pedal-bicycle; one canoe or kayak up to 16 ft (5 m) long; up to 20 records or tapes; linen for personal use, small amount of kitchen utensils, folding table and chairs.

Pets: you may take your dog or cat into Mexico with a veterinary's certificate of good health in duplicate. Dogs must have a certificate of inoculation against rabies and distemper, dated within the last 3 months and notarized by the Mexican consul in the area in which the certificate was issued. Pets are more suitable for camping holidays as few hotels will accept animals and they are not permitted on first class buses. Airlines and train services require pets to travel in kennels in a special compartment.

It is strictly forbidden to take in fresh fruit, vegetables, pork and dairy products, plants, flowers and, above all, narcotics.

All United States residents returning home who have been out of the country for more than 48 hours may bring in $400 retail value of purchases for personal use or as gifts including up to 200 cigarettes and 100 cigars (non-Cuban). Citizens who are 21 or older may bring in 1 liter (33.8 fl oz) of alcohol without having to pay duty. Certain craft items can be taken into the United States duty-free which exceed the $400 limit, including ceramics, pottery, costume jewelry, some furniture, metal decorative items, onyx products, wood carvings, papier maché.

You may not bring back narcotics, meats, fruit, vegetables, plants, soil or other agricultural items. If your pet has been out of the country for more than 30 days, it will require an inoculation certificate to re-enter.

U.K. citizens returning home (over the age of 17) are allowed the following items duty-free: up to 200 cigarettes or 100 cigarillos or 50 cigars or 250 grams of pipe tobacco; 2 litres of still wine; 1 litre of 38.8° plus proof or 2 litres of less than 38.8° proof alcohol or 2 litres of fortified or sparkling wine; all U.K. citizens may bring home 50 grams of perfume; 250 cc (9 fl oz) of toilet water. You may also bring in £28 retail value of goods purchased in the form of gifts or for personal use without paying duty.

No animal (dead or alive) may be brought directly into the country. All pets must enter a six month quarantine. No animal is exempt from this, even if already inoculated.

Canadians returning home, who have been outside Canada for at least seven days, may bring in a reasonable number of personal effects. Upon written declaration, you can claim an exemption of $300 import duty a year plus, if the province through which you return to Canada permits it, an allowance of 200 cigarettes, 50 cigars, 2 lbs of tobacco and 1.1 liters of liquor. Further details are obtainable from the Canada Customs leaflet, 'I Declare'.

All visitors: any authentic archaeological pieces, colonial art or other artifacts cannot be exported from Mexico. The export of gold and silver coins is also restricted.

If you plan to bring several items home, it is advisable to check first with Mexican customs.

CURRENCY

The unit of currency in Mexico is the *peso*. Paper bills *(billetes)* to the value of 50, 100, 500, 1,000, 5,000 and 10,000 pesos are issued and coins *(monedas)* to the value of

1, 5, 10, 20 and 50 pesos. Coins of smaller value are minted in 10, 20 and 50 *centavos* but the 10 and 50 coins are practically out of circulation now. Since the devaluations of 1982 the peso has fluctuated daily and the rate of exchange for the day is posted at banks or exchange counters. At the time of writing the exchange rate was approximately 225 pesos to the U.S. dollar but this could have altered considerably in the meantime. Do take note that certain items in Mexico can be quoted in U.S. dollars rather than Mexican pesos, hotel rates for instance. Figures quoted in pesos should be followed by MN (*Moneda Nacional* — national currency) and dollars by US$, but it is always wise to check first.

Banks normally offer the best exchange rate but they are not always open and major hotels and airports also provide exchange facilities. Banking hours vary. Most are open from 9 am to 1.30 pm, Monday to Friday and some larger banks also open from 4-6 pm. You will sometimes find one open in the mornings and afternoons on Saturdays and even on Sunday mornings, but do not count on it. Try to avoid Fridays when you may have a long wait. Your passport or proper identification must be shown when changing travelers checks. Those most widely recognized are American Express, Thomas Cook, Citicorp, Visa and MasterCard.

European visitors are advised to take travelers checks in U.S. dollars rather than in European currency as there can be difficulties in changing European currency. When changing money always ask what the going rate is (this can change daily) and check carefully that you have received the correct amount.

Well-known credit cards are widely accepted in tourist centers and big cities. In other areas, they are generally accepted by large hotels, restaurants of a certain standard, retail stores, airlines and car rental companies. The following cards are most widely recognized in Mexico: American Express, Diners Club, Carte Blanche, MasterCard, Visa. Try not to carry around large amounts of cash and keep it separate from your checks. Do not handle cash carelessly or openly show a large roll of notes. As with traveling in any country take good care of your money and try to guard against pick-pockets.

HOW TO GET THERE

By air: Mexico receives around 600 international flights every week from many parts of the world. About 450 of these are from the United States. There are international airports in the following cities: Mexico City, Acapulco, Cancún, Cozumel, Ixtapa/Zihuatanejo, Guaymas, Guadalajara, La Paz, Hermosillo, Mazatlán, Mérida, Monterrey, Puerto Vallarta.

There are direct flights to Mexico City and other Mexican destinations from major cities in the United States and connections are available from most others. You can travel directly by air from Albuquerque, Atlanta, Boston, Chicago, Dallas/Fort Worth, Denver, Detroit, El Paso, Houston, Kansas City, Los Angeles, Miami, New Orleans, New York, Philadelphia, Phoenix, San Antonio, San Francisco, Tucson and Washington but you should check with your travel agent as this information is subject to change. Numerous charters and package tours are available. Leading airlines with regular scheduled services from the United States to Mexico City and other cities include: Air France, American Airlines, British Airways, Continental, Eastern, Frontier, Hughes, Airwest, Lacsa, Lufthansa, Northwest Orient, Pan American, Republic, United, Western Airlines, and the two Mexican National Airlines, Aeroméxico and Mexicana. Tariffs and schedules change constantly and there are changes likely in the range of airlines available. Again it is best to check with your travel agent or with the airlines.

This also applies to information about flights from the United Kingdom from where there are various ways of reaching Mexico City. You can travel Pan American via Miami or New York and Houston; KLM via Amsterdam; American Airlines via Dallas (with connections to several destinations in Mexico); Air France via Paris; Iberia via Madrid. British Airways fly to Miami, Chicago, New York and Los Angeles and British Caledonian to Houston and Dallas which serve as good United States gateways for connections with other airlines to Mexico. There are scheduled flights between Canada and Mexico from Calgary, Montréal and Vancouver, served by Pan American, Iberia, Air Canada and Japan Airlines. Charters are also available. This information is also subject to change.

Fares: before committing yourself, you should check with a good travel agent as he may be able to recommend cheaper or discount flights to Mexico. Prices vary according to the season. The high season is in winter. ITX and APEX tickets are cheaper but bear in mind that they can be subject to various conditions and some tickets may not be refundable or they may have to be purchased in advance. Fares range from first-class to economy ticket and some airlines offer the opportunity to travel further south after stopping off in

Mexico City for a few nights. Before making plans, remember that Mexican weather is fine all year in many areas.

By sea: increasing numbers of cruise ships are connecting the United States with Mexico by sea. Cruises from San Francisco and Los Angeles sail down the Pacific coast of Mexico stopping at popular destinations such as Cabo San Lucas, Mazatlán, Puerto Vallarta, Manzanillo, Ixtapa/Zihuatanejo and Acapulco. From Florida there are cruises operating regularly to the Yucatán peninsula with stops at Cozumel and Cancún. There are also cruises from New York through the Panama Canal to Acapulco. Private yachts and sailboats can enter the country at a number of ports. (Information available from Mexican Tourist offices or travel agents.)

By car: many Americans travel to Mexico by car, particularly those living in the border states. There are seven major entry points from the United States. One of the most famous is Tijuana. From here the Transpeninsula Highway leads through Baja California, stretching for 1050 miles (1690 km) down to the southernmost point at Cabo San Lucas, with ferry connections to the mainland at certain points. (Ferries cross from Santa Rosalia to Guaymas, from Pichilingue near La Paz to Topolobampo, Los Mochis and Mazatlán and from Cabo San Lucas to Puerto Vallarta.) The other main border crossing points are: Nogales — 1423 miles (2290 km) down the western route to Mexico City; El Paso/Ciudad Juarez following the west-central highway 1131 miles (1820 km) to Mexico City; Eagle Pass/Piedras Negras central route to capital 784 miles (1262 km); Laredo/Nuevo Laredo 757 miles (1218 km) taking the central route; McAllen/Reynosa 691 miles (1112 km) or Brownsville/Matamoros 630 miles (1014 km) taking the eastern route to Mexico City. For details of traveling around by car and insurance, see 'If you are Driving', p. 17.

By rail: Mexico has an extensive railroad network. If traveling to Mexico from the United States you must change at the Mexican border onto their national railroad system. It is difficult to obtain reservations beforehand as few travel agents in the United States handle rail bookings. Once you are in Mexico you can reserve at the station of departure. From all over the United States and Canada, connections can be made (sometimes involving a short bus journey) with Mexican rail services which leave from the border points of Nogales, Mexicali, Ciudad Acuña, Matamoros, Ciudad Juárez and Nuevo Laredo, for Mexico City and other major cities in Mexico. The National Railways of Mexico issues revised timetables of dates, times etc every year. Rail travel in Mexico is not very expensive.

By bus: United States bus lines connect with the Mexican services at all main entry points with first class services run by private companies to destinations all over the country. (See p. 16 for more detailed information.) Tours by bus are also available from the United States into Mexico with Greyhound and Continental Trailways. Bus travel can be very time-consuming if you are making a long journey from the United States but it is very economical.

Package tours: an economical and convenient way of getting to know the country, especially for a first visit. There are numerous tours available from the United States to Mexico, many from Canada, and, to a lesser extent, from the United Kingdom. Travel agents will provide you with information on package tours available. You should then study the brochures very carefully and find out which amenities and services are included in the price before booking.

INTERNAL TRAVEL

Domestic flights: Mexico has an excellent air network within the country. There are flights to every major city and tourist center, served by Mexico's two national airlines, *Aeroméxico* and *Mexicana de Aviación*. More remote areas can be reached by small regional airlines. Large distances and often mountainous terrain encourages air travel to be widely used. As flights are frequently full it is advisable to book in advance whenever possible. The National Airlines do not compete financially with one another and each has its own designated list of destinations although some of these do overlap. More important routes have several daily flights, while less popular journeys take place once per day or a few times per week. There is only one class of accommodation. Excursion fares are available on some routes. On round-trip journeys you usually buy two one way tickets. Internal fares were very reasonable but, as a result of high inflation in recent times, there have been some increases. *Aeroméxico* and *Mexicana* both provide a daily 45 minute shuttle service from Mexico City to Acapulco.

Ferries: there are a number of regular ferry services connecting the west coast ports of Mexico across to lower Baja California, and you can take your car. Return services include: Mazatlán to La Paz,

Topolobampo to Pichilingue near La Paz, Puerto Vallarta to Cabo San Lucas, Guaymas to Santa Rosalia and Guaymas to La Paz. As frequencies and timings can vary, it's best to check details beforehand with your travel agent. Advance reservations are recommended as ferries are usually busy and even if you have a reservation, you should arrive at the ferry terminal on the morning of the day of departure to purchase your ticket.

There are also ferries between the Caribbean ports. Car ferries leave from Puerto Morelos for Cozumel, from Playa Carmen to Cozumel and from Punta Sam (just north of Cancún) for Isla Mujeres. There is a passenger-only service from Puerto Juárez (north of Cancún) to Isla Mujeres and a hydrofoil ferry between Cancún and Cozumel. Tickets can usually be obtained on the spot.

Railways: the national railway system is called Ferrocarriles Nacionales de México. There are some 15,000 miles of track in Mexico extending all over the country, from United States border entry points down to Central America. Rail travel is inexpensive, but journeys are very lengthy and frequently unpunctual, so allow for plenty of time. Mexico City is served by trains from the border towns of Mexicali, Nogales, Ciudad Juárez, Piedras Negras, Nuevo Laredo and Matamoros. At the border you change onto Mexican railways where it is advisable to take first-class if you wish to travel in comfort. This is much cheaper than in the United States and a sleeper compartment costs little more than the ordinary fare. Many long distance trains have pullman sleepers with single compartments, double bedrooms or a suite with 3 or more beds. There are dining and observation cars and most have air conditioning. Some have dormitory cars, *dormitorios*, in which the beds are surrounded by curtains. Stopovers are permitted if you have a first class ticket, provided the ticket is marked accordingly by the ticket clerk at the point of purchase. Rail timetables are issued in Mexico, but always re-check timings.

Special rail journey: the spectacular Copper Canyon Route *(Ferrocarril de Chihuahua al Pacífico)*, from Ojinaga, on the United States border through Chihuahua down to the Pacific Coast, is often called the 'world's most scenic railroad'. The construction grew out of the dream of Albert K. Owen, a citizen of the United States. After many years of frustrated attempts to get the project off the ground Mexican engineers finally declared, in 1953, that they were ready to commence. This remarkable technical feat was accomplished in 1961. The line covers 403 miles (650 km) of deep 5000 ft (1520 m) gorges and heights 8000 ft (2440 m) above sea level. While the line starts in the frontier town of Ojinaga, the main boarding point is Chihuahua, and the line ends at the pacific ports of Los Mochis and Topolobampo. The train climbs endless miles of rugged peaks and reaches a height of over 8600 ft (2600 m) at a point called Los Ojitos (the little eyes). A ride on the Barranca del Cobre (Copper Canyon) route can last a whole day. The journey is breathtaking and it rivals the Grand Canyon for beauty. There are several places at which you can stop overnight, or longer, to visit the spectacular surroundings. These include Copper Canyon Lodge which is in Tarahumara Indian country. An estimated 40,000 Tarahumara Indians live among the wild sierras. These cave dwellers are among Mexico's most primitive and isolated tribes and are of great ethnographic interest. Organized expeditions are available to Indian villages, canyons and waterfalls and you can make some trips on horseback. There are other places with accommodations for stopping off such as at Creel and Divisadero. The stop at El Divisadero (the look-out) affords a magnificent view over the mountain ranges and deep gorges. In its gradual descent to the coast, the train passes across the plain through areas of conifers and shrubs. It is most rewarding to make the trip from Los Mochis to Chihuahua, rather than in the reverse direction, as you will pass through the most scenic part of the journey in daylight. The train is air-conditioned and has a bar and restaurant car. Check with your agent for timings.

Local buses: bus travel in Mexico can be most enjoyable, especially if you are interested in the more unusual tourist destinations. Privately owned companies operate services to all parts of the country. They work efficiently on the whole and prices are very reasonable. There are regular services from major United States points of entry down to Mexico City. Continental Trailways and Greyhound provide a number of unescorted bus tours from the United States into Mexico including round trips to many destinations.

Numerous lines, extending down to Guatemala and Belize (from the Yucatán), take you to destinations all over the country. For long distance travel, it is advisable to use only deluxe and first-class service for comfort. There is little difference in cost and these generally have in-bus toilets, air conditioning, and are sometimes accompanied by stewards. If you are not traveling directly to your final destination, you must buy your ticket in segments as one-way tickets only are sold which do not allow for stopovers.

Mexico City has four bus terminals serving travel to the north, south, east and west. Most towns and sizeable villages have a terminal with a choice of many daily services. Even some remote places have surprisingly modern terminals.

Country buses, running between local villages are usually crammed full and pick up passengers along the route. Seats are generally wooden and you can find yourself traveling alongside chickens and farm animals on some buses. In rural areas, bus travel can be fun but if you are traveling independently it is helpful to have some knowledge of Spanish. Travelers in more remote areas should take care and it is best not to stray too far from civilization if you are on your own.

Taxis: available in all towns and centers of any size. They are always lined up to take you into town from airports and can be hired for traveling around town by the hour or by the day. Prices should always be agreed upon before departure. For information on taxi services in Mexico City see p. 42.

Organized excursions: it is possible to join a tour starting from Mexico City. There are plenty available, ranging from half-day, full day or longer trips to other parts of the country. For local tours, information is available at major hotels and from travel agents.

By car: for information on traveling by car in Mexico see 'If you are Driving'.

IF YOU ARE DRIVING

Driving is a good way of traveling independently and exploring the country. Mexico has more than 120,000 miles (190,000 km) of road and, with government investment, the highway system is growing rapidly.

License: the valid driving license of a United States, British or Canadian citizen is acceptable in Mexico but it is best to have an International Driving License. You must also have a car permit. This can be obtained at the United States—Mexico border point, free of charge upon presentation of the car's registration and/or proof of ownership and it is issued for the same period of time as your tourist card (see p.12). If driving a rented car or a vehicle belonging to someone else, you must have a notarized affidavit authorizing you to drive the car. Citizens of the United Kingdom who are renting a car will need an International Driving Permit which can be obtained through the AA or RAC. The same applies to a trailer. It is illegal for visitors to sell their cars in Mexico and, should you need to leave the country without your car, it must be left in bond at the airport, for a period only as long as the validity of your tourist card.

Insurance: as your car insurance will not cover you in Mexico, you should buy Mexican insurance. This can be arranged through leading companies in the United States which handle Mexican insurance, or in towns near the Mexican border where there are many such agents. If you cut your visit short a refund will be paid. It is advisable to buy the most comprehensive policy available to ensure that your car is fully covered for liability, property damage, physical liability and theft.

Road safety and highway conditions: Mexicans drive on the right-hand side of the road. There are some four-lane highways, but the majority are two-lane and, except for remote areas, they are generally well surfaced. Four-lane superhighways are usually quite expensive toll roads, but they do allow you to get to your destination quickly. Distances are measured in kilometers and speed limits are usually around 80 to 100 kilometers per hour (approx. 50 to 60 mph). City speed limits can be very low and they are not always observed by Mexicans, but visitors are advised to obey them. It may be helpful to know that a speed limit of 40 kph is roughly 25 mph and 30 kph is roughly 18 mph.

Most cities have a number of one-way streets. Signs on each corner indicate the direction by an arrow. Two-way streets have an arrow with two points. Watch out for the *topes*, which are small concrete or steel domes set in some streets to make you slow right down. Hitting one, even at slow speeds, can be quite a bump. Try to avoid driving after dark. Visibility is often poor and, as fields are not fenced in, cattle or other animals can stray onto the road. Other vehicles do not always use their headlights and bicycles often have no lights. You will occasionally come across a one-lane bridge on a two-lane highway. The Mexican procedure for this is to slow right down and the driver who flashes his lights first has the priority to cross.

Precautions: whether driving your own car or a rented one, it is wise to make sure that your car is in top order and that the brakes have been checked before setting out. It is very important to ensure that the tires are suitable for the trip. They should be fairly new and of the best quality as they will probably have to withstand potholes in the rainy season or longer journeys than usual, possibly over different terrain. Carry as many spare parts as possible, a jack, and water for the radiator, particularly if you are traveling in remote areas. Particularly if you are alone, it is best to take care and avoid remote areas where you are more vulnerable to those Mexicans who are less scrupulous.

Breakdown: in case of breakdown, it's best to carry flares or reflectors and a white rag for signaling. If your car does break down, pull off the road, raise the hood of your car as a signal that you need assistance and tie a white rag to some part of the vehicle. Major highways are constantly patrolled by a fleet of emergency service trucks, called the 'Green Angels' and so there is no need to take the risk of leaving your car unattended. Green Angels are government-controlled and manned by crews who speak English. They carry equipment, make minor repairs and offer information or they will tow your car and they can provide first aid. The service is free and you are charged only for the cost of spare parts, gas, oil, etc. Green Angels and Pemex stations should be able to direct you to a good mechanic.

Accidents: if you witness an accident, do not stop immediately. You should notify the first policeman you encounter or one of the Green Angels, but make sure you are away from the scene of the accident. Witnesses of accidents are often held in jail by the police to prevent them from disappearing and until responsibility for the accident has been established.

If you are involved in a car accident, do not call the police unless strictly necessary. Do not admit liability and try to persuade witnesses, if you can, to stay and give evidence, although this might be difficult. If the other driver is insured, exchange details and contact your insurance company as soon as you can. If you have a rented car, you should call the number given in the rental contract.

Police uniforms vary throughout the country. In Mexico City, traffic and civil police wear powder blue uniforms and parking police dress in khaki. Traffic laws are not consistently enforced and you can try arguing your way out of it but it is usually best to pay up, especially if the alternative is a trip to the police station. Cars parked illegally can sometimes be removed by the police or the license plates taken away. This requires a trip to the police station and the payment of a fine *(una multa).* Parking meters have been installed in the central areas of Mexico City and large cities. Do not leave valuables or any goods in your car unless they are stowed away in the trunk. They will be safer at your hotel or home. Lock the car doors and, whenever possible, park in garages or special parking lots. These are usually frequented by young boys who offer to keep an eye on your car for a small tip. It is wise to accept.

Pemex is the only brand of gasoline and oil sold in Mexico since the petroleum industry was nationalized in 1938. There are two grades of gas available, the more expensive Extra, from silver pumps and Nova, from the blue pumps.

Renting a car: a valid license is required for car rental (see 'license', p. 17). Prices vary from one rental company to another. The leading companies such as Hertz, Avis and Budget usually charge 'international prices', and can be booked in advance from your home country. Local firms can charge lower prices but think carefully before renting from an unknown firm. Payment is usually made by credit card. Remember that some agencies impose minimum age limit of 25 years or older. Insurance, which is compulsory, is arranged through the rental company. Check any rented car thoroughly before setting off, making sure necessary equipment, such as spare tire and tools, are there. Mopeds and bicycles can be rented at most popular resorts.

Some useful words for the motorist:
alto stop
despacio slow
peligro danger
Precaución warning
ceda el paso give right of way
curva curve
tránsito circulación one way (usually marked with an arrow)
estacionamiento parking (usually abbreviated by large E)
conserve su derecha keep to the right.

A large E with a bar drawn across it means 'no parking'. When a policeman is directing traffic; if he faces you or turns his back, remain stationary until he turns to the side. Try to arm yourself with a good map before departure and alway check that you have enough gas as in some areas there are very few gas stations.

WHERE TO STAY

Mexico offers a complete range of accommodations to suit all tastes and in every price category. The enormous growth of tourism in recent years has been reflected by the increase in hotel construction and there are continuing plans for new developments to meet the demand.

You can find top luxury hotels in major cities and popular tourist resorts. Most are controlled by international chains including such groups as Westin, Sheraton,

Where to Stay

Hyatt and Holiday Inn. Many hotels are situated in lovely grounds and can offer additional facilities such as golf, tennis, swimming and, in seaside resorts, water sports. Hotels in this category can be expensive in tourist centers during the high season (roughly from December to April) when rates are higher. During peak periods, some hotels require you to take MAP (Modified American Plan) which includes breakfast and one other meal.

Medium-priced hotel chains run by leading Mexican groups such as Aristos, El Presidente, Posadas de Mexico, Krystal, Calinda Quality hotels, Mision and Viva have many properties throughout Mexico. The American chain, Best Western, has a number of attractive hotels in different centers. Hotels within this price range generally have pleasant, fairly large rooms with a shower and/or a bath. There is usually a restaurant, bar, air conditioning in certain areas and some additional facilities. Hotels normally employ at least one member of staff who speaks English. Prices are quite reasonable in general.

You can find inexpensive accommodations in most cities and in less frequented tourist spots. Even in modest hotels you can usually book a room with a shower. It's best to have a look at your room before checking in as standards can vary considerably.

In the central highlands of the country particularly, there are many beautiful colonial-style hotels, converted from genuine old Spanish haciendas. Rooms are usually large and tastefully decorated. Many of these hotels are set in picturesque grounds and offer swimming and other sports activities such as tennis, golf etc. There are a number of spa resorts, also mainly in this region, which offer attractive accommodations, thermal baths, beauty treatment and many recreational activities. Numerous United States-style motels are located outside cities along main highways, particularly in the north. These are usually inexpensive and convenient for motorists who wish to make overnight stops.

Many resorts and tourist centers have attractive hotel complexes which are constructed as picturesque holiday villages. Some have bungalow-type accommodations suitable for individuals or families. Each bungalow has its own private pool or operates on a share-pool basis. Outstanding examples of this type of accommodations are to be found in Acapulco, Puerto Vallarta and along the coastline south of Puerto Vallarta.

Unless you book well in advance it is often difficult to get a room for top resorts during peak seasons such as Christmas, Easter and the holiday period in September. Resorts and inland centers, especially those within range of Mexico City, are also often full at weekends. If you can avoid these times it is usually fairly easy to find a room, especially in less frequented tourist areas.

Hotel rates are set and approved by the Tourism Secretariat, who publish a list of ratings, from 1-star to 5-stars. Room rates should be posted in your room but as is often the case in Mexico, don't depend on it! It is always wise to check your room rate before signing in. Remember that 15% federal tax (IVA) is added to all hotel bills. Tips are left to your discretion (for suggestions, see 'Tipping' p. 30). Single travelers are unfortunately at a disadvantage, in terms of cost, as many hotels have only double rooms and single occupancy will cost you nearly as much, if not the same, as for two people.

It is best to make your reservations through a reputable travel agent. Depending upon the particular circumstances, deposits may be required or even full payment in advance. Make sure you have confirmation before departure and the necessary vouchers. Rooms are usually held until 6 pm. If you think that there is a chance you may arrive later than this, let the hotel know. Check-out time varies, but you should usually have vacated the room by 2 pm. Recognized credit cards are acceptable for making payment in top class hotels.

Extra beds for young children in your room may be included free or there may be a small charge. This depends upon each particular hotel.

At main coastal resorts you can rent self-contained fully furnished condominiums and apartments, for short or longer periods. One leading operator is Playasol, which has large condominiums in Acapulco, Puerto Vallarta, Manzanillo and Cancún. Your travel agent should have up-to-date information on finding a villa or a flat.

Mexico City offers a number of kitchenette-apartment suites with one or more bedrooms. You can rent them for short periods but they are particularly convenient for visitors planning to stay for some time. Furnished apartments with a maid service are also available. Your travel agent may be able to put you in touch with rental agents and there are a number of publications carrying advertisements which you may find in your hotel room or at travel agencies in Mexico.

There are numerous trailer parks and camping grounds all over Mexico. For more information please see the camping section of 'Enjoy Yourself', p. 22.

FOOD AND DRINK

The popular notion that all Mexican food is red-hot and fiery is a complete misconception. Genuine Mexican cuisine is a unique combination of native Indian and Spanish traditions, with some French and even Oriental influences. While some dishes can be hot and spicy, it is often the accompanying, optional chillie-based sauces which provide the hot, piquant, element. In fact much of Mexico's authentic cuisine is mild, characterized by the subtle use of spices and delicate flavors. Various regions have their own specialties and typical cuisine can vary greatly from north to south. Authentic Yucatecan cuisine is generally delicate and fragrant rather than hot, even though this is the home of the fiery *chile habanero* — the hottest chilli in Mexico. The cuisine of Guadalajara and Puebla is rich and colorful, with strong colonial traditions. Coastal areas offer a wide selection of excellent fresh seafood and the north, although lacking in traditional dishes, is renowned for the quality of its beef.

Maize and beans have been basic ingredients in Mexico since they were first cultivated hundreds of years ago, and they remain so today. The Spaniards gave the name of *tortilla* to the thin, corn pancakes which form the basis for countless recipes. (Original name was tlaxcali, from Tlaxcala). Mexican tortillas, served on their own, are eaten like bread as an accompaniment to the meal. Stuffed with beef, chicken, pork, cheese, avocado etc, rolled and fried, they become *tacos*, and can be eaten as snacks or as a main dish. When topped with a sauce and baked, they are called *enchiladas*. *Enchiladas suizas* is a popular dish of *tortillas* filled with chicken and topped with a sauce of chillies, cream and cheese. *Tamales* are made from the same dough, filled with chicken or meat, wrapped in corn husks and steamed.

Mexican dishes are often accompanied by *guacamole* (mashed avocado with chopped raw tomato, onion, chillie and flavored with fresh coriander) and *refritos* (beans mashed and fried). You can ask separately for hot sauces, which the Mexicans describe as *picante*, to sprinkle over your dish.

If you are offered *tostadas, chalupas, nachos, quesadillas* or *gorditas*, they are all formed from tortillas and filled or topped with traditional Mexican ingredients such as chillies, tomatoes and beans. Tostadas are crisp and most are fried.

Starters are varied and tasty. Called *botanas* or *antojitos*, which means literally 'little whims', they are delicious to nibble over your aperitif. Many tortilla-based dishes are served in small portions to be taken as snacks. Tasty pieces of pork, known as *carnitas* also make a good starter.

Of the countless dishes which form part of traditional Mexican cooking, only a limited number feature on restaurant menus in those areas most frequented by tourists. Many recipes consist of numerous ingredients and involve hours, if not days, of preparation and you are only likely to come across some of these very traditional dishes in Mexican restaurants serving a small local population or in the home. Most restaurants do serve tortilla-based dishes such as *tacos* and *tamales* with *guacamole* and *refritos*. Some of the Mexican dishes more commonly produced for the tourist include *ceviche acapulqueño* — marinated fish in limejuice; *coctel de camarones* or *coctel de ostiones* — seafood cocktails with Mexican-style sauce; blanco de Pátzcuaro — delicately flavored white fish from Lake Pátzcuaro, served with wedges of lime.

Mexico is renowned for delicious homemade soups which you can get in some restaurants. Favorites are: *sopa de tortilla* — tortilla soup; *sopa de frijol* — bean soup; *sopa de aguacate* — avocado soup; *pozole* — thick soup of pork basis; *sopa de flor de calabaza* — pumpkin blossom soup.

Mole poblano is considered a national dish and it is served on special and festive occasions. There are over 30 ingredients in this rich dark sauce, including chillies, spices and unsweetened chocolate. The sauce, which is usually served with turkey or chicken complements the meat very well. Unsweetened chocolate is a popular ingredient used in many dishes. The effect is subtle and well worth tasting. *Chiles rellenos* are long green peppers stuffed with minced chicken, other meats or cheese and fried. It is then simmered in tomato sauce before being served. *Carne asada* is grilled meat which is often tough but it is tasty. *Huachinango a la veracruzana* is red snapper baked in a sauce of tomatoes, olives and onions. Chicken or pork *'pipian'* is a rich sauce of tomatoes, chillies and sesame seeds.

Mexico has a tremendous variety of seafood such as lobster, crab, giant prawns, oysters and excellent fish. Seafood is best eaten in coastal resorts or in top class restaurants in large cities. The freshest seafood is often served in modest local beachfront restaurants.

Desserts are usually very sweet, mostly based on eggs, milk and sugar; among the most popular are *cajeta* (a toffee candy), *flan* (custard) and ice cream.

You can buy delicious tropical fruit such as mango, pineapple, papya and melon. At seaside resorts, many hotels serve delicious platers of assorted fruits and you can find freshly squeezed orange juice in most hotels.

A typical Mexican breakfast can become a huge meal. Favorites are *huevos revueltos a la Mexicana* (scrambled eggs with onion, chillies and tomatoes), *huevos rancheros* (fried eggs served on a tortilla with red chille sauce), *chilaquiles* (filling dish consisting of pieces of tortilla, eggs and chillies).

Soft drinks are called *refrescos* and all sorts of flavors are available, fizzy or otherwise. Fruit juices are called *jugo de fruta*. *Cidral* is a popular apple based drink.

Mineral water is always available, often listed by the brand name *Tehuacán* which is regarded as the best in Mexico. You can buy mineral water still (sin gas) or sparkling (con gas).

Coffee is produced in the southeastern areas of Mexico. The Mexicans have a way of preparing it brewed with cinnamon and sugar and served in small earthenware cups. If you would like to try this, ask for *café de olla*. If you would prefer coffee as you drink it at home, the best available is *café americano*. An increasing number of restaurants now offer expresso or cappuccino coffee as well. You may enjoy *café con leche* which is often served in a tall glass and consists of a mixture of strong coffee and hot milk. Hot chocolate is a great favorite with Mexicans, often served with a touch of cinnamon. For tea drinkers, one of the most pleasant aromatic teas is *te de manzanilla*.

Mexico's most famous drink is *tequila* — a strong alcoholic drink made from the distilled juice of the *agave tequiliana* plant which grows in Jalisco. You can take it 'straight', the 'Mexican way' with a pinch of salt and lime juice or in any number of cocktails. The margarita cocktail and tequila sunrise are popular drinks, not only in Mexico, but in many sophisticated hotel bars throughout the world. *Commemorativo tequila* is golden-colored and smooth-tasting. *Mezcal* from Oaxaca is also very potent and it, too, is produced from the agave plant. Pulque, which is very nourishing, is mildly alcoholic and was used as a sacred drink by the Aztecs. Local men congregate in *pulquería* bars to drink pulque. These bars are similar to *cantinas* and women are unlikely to be made welcome!

Kahlua is a pleasant tasting coffee-based liqueur. Rum and brandy are also produced in Mexico. Brandy and Coca-Cola is a popular Mexican combination. *Ron Castillo* and *Bacardi* are favorite brands of rum and are used to make popular cocktails such as Planters Punch and Cuba Libre. Vodka is distilled by several companies. Excellent beer is produced in many different parts of the country. There are two varieties — dark *(oscura)* and light *(clara)* and popular brands include *Negra Modelo, Dos Equis, Tres Equis* (oscura) and *Bohémia*. Mexico is not traditionally a wine-drinking country but an increasing number of local wines are appearing on the market and quality is improving. They are mostly produced in Baja California and the central regions of Mexico, around Querétaro and Hidalgo states. It is becoming more fashionable to take wine with the meal in sophisticated restaurants. Imported French wine is available but it is very expensive.

Mexican food and drink is excellent but there are a few precautions all travelers should take: it is wise not to over eat or consume too much alcohol at high altitudes. In Mexico City, for example, which is over 7000 ft above sea-level, alcohol can have an increased intoxicating effect as the air gets thinner. It is best to avoid tap water or, if possible, anything that has been washed in it. Good hotels should provide a bottle of purified water in your room. If not, request one. Peel all fruit before eating it, and only eat salads at top class restaurants in major cities or resorts. Avoid unpasteurised milk. Beware of stopping at any of the numerous roadside taco vendors for a tasty snack, however tempting, unless the place is known to you or recommended by someone local. Be wary of pork in hot, tropical regions.

When eating out remember that many restaurants do not open their doors until about 1 pm as Mexicans tend not to start their midday meal until well after this. It is not uncommon for lunches to go on for hours! Dinner usually starts from about 8 or 9 pm. As fashionable restaurants are invariably full, it is safer to reserve a table in advance.

In Mexico City, major towns and popular resorts, you will find a wide variety of restaurants catering to every taste and offering international and Mexican cuisine. Restaurants vary tremendously in price. For more details of eating out in Mexico see 'Mexico City', p. 48. Formality of dress is expected in good restaurants but casual wear is more common in coastal resorts.

There are no laws prohibiting drinking in Mexico, but there is an exception at voting time, which happens once every six years when the Mexicans go to the polls to vote for the new President. From Friday night to Sunday night the *Ley Seca* literally 'dry law', comes into effect and no liquor can be sold in restaurants or stores during this period.

ENJOY YOURSELF

Bullfighting: a very popular sport in Mexico and most major cities have a Plaza de Toros (bull ring). The 'Big season', when experienced matadors fight, is from December to April and the little season, when novices perform, is between September and December. (In some border towns the seasons are in reverse.) Some of the prominent Spanish matadors often fight during the main season on Sundays and on fiesta days. There are fights most Sundays in Mexico City, commencing at 4.30 pm. Tickets can usually be obtained from your hotel, travel agencies or at the ring. Cheaper seats are in the sun *(sol)* and better seats are on the shady side *(sombra)* which is more comfortable to view from. There are bullrings in Guadalajara, border towns and all over central Mexico, with fights on Sundays and during local fiestas.

Camping: there are campsites and trailer parks along major highways and on the outskirts of all major towns. Facilities usually include hot showers, toilets, a laundromat and have a nearby store for provisions. Drinking water should be boiled or purified. Details and lists of sites can be obtained from most tourist offices, or by purchasing special publications. Rand McNally *Campgrounds and Trailer Parks*, with an extensive section on Mexico, is very helpful. It is not advisable to park your trailer or camper overnight along the roadside or in any isolated spot away from civilization. A number of National Parks with magnificent scenery have areas set aside for camping and backpackers.

Charreadas: this Mexican-style rodeo is a most enjoyable and colorful event. Performances are held most Sunday mornings in Mexico City, Guadalajara, and in most towns and villages around the central and northwest regions. Amateur 'cowboys' and 'cowgirls' demonstrate their skills of horsemanship. Young girls, dressed in gaily colored costumes ride sidesaddle as they perform with great expertize. There are frequent interruptions for exhibitions of regional dancing and singing, and ballet on horseback. Your travel agent or hotel will give you details and help you to get tickets.

Cruising: a number of cruise liners offer trips from California down the 'Mexican Riviera' calling in at popular destinations such as Manzanillo, Ixtapa/Zihuatanejo, Puerto Vallarta, Acapulco and Cabo San Lucas. From Florida there are trips to the Caribbean coast of Mexico, with stops at Cozumel and Cancún. Your travel agent will have further information.

Fishing (sea): Mexico's magnificent coast line offers some of the best deep-sea fishing in the world. Fishermen from the United States in particular, travel great distances down the Baja California peninsula or journey to the Caribbean coast to fish for marlin, sailfish, snook, bass, red snapper, dorado, pompano and shark. All major ports and resorts have charter boats and fishing gear for hire. A fishing permit is required and can be obtained for a small fee from any fishing facility, local wildlife warden, the harbor master or from local offices of the Secretaría de Industry y Comercio. Fishing equipment can be brought into the country without customs duties being payable. Temporary permits are issued for boats and trailers entering Mexico. A small fee is charged according to the weight of your vehicle. For more information on regulations and dates of fishing tournaments you can write to the Sub-Dirección de Aquafición secretaria de Turismo, Presidente Masaryk 172, 6th Floor, Mexico DF 1156.

Fresh water fishing: Mexico abounds in lakes, rivers, lagoons and reservoirs and visitors often spend days fishing for catfish, trout, carp, black bass and whitefish. It is best to bring your own tackle, as equipment for rent is not always readily available.

Golf: there are many superb golf courses in Mexico, particularly in Mexico City, Guadalajara, Acapulco, Cancún, Ixtapa, Manzanillo and some inland resorts. In major towns, it is difficult to get a game unless you are invited as a guest by members of local golf clubs. If your hotel is connected with a golf course, you will find it much easier. At coastal resorts and some inland resorts, tourists can usually gain access to local courses. At weekends the demand is usually greater. Facilities vary but most have clubs, golf carts and caddies for hire if required. The courses themselves can be very picturesque and most players will find that they present an interesting and scenic challenge.

Horseback riding: horses are available for hire in many places including National Parks, beach resorts, inland tourist centers and on the outskirts of most large cities. You can ride on your own or accompanied by an instructor. Expeditions can be joined in various parts of the country, from the wild and rugged sierras in the north, to the lush jungle areas of the south. There are some outstanding organized trips into the spectacular Copper Canyon from El Divisadero (Chihuahua

Surfing at Puerto Escondido

state). Further south you can ride through the jungles and Indian villages near San Cristóbal de las Casas (Chiapas).

For information on stables and specialist riding holidays, write to Federación Ecuestre Méxicana, Cda. Ahumada 31, México DF.

Hunting: Mexican countryside provides excellent opportunities for hunting in such varied terrain as the Sierra Madres in the north and the dense jungle areas of Chiapas and the Yucatán in the south. Game includes wild boar, lynx, deer and wolf, and many species of wild fowl such as dove, wild turkey, duck, quail and grouse. Bringing guns into the country and then taking them home with you can depend upon a long administrative process. Mexico does not encourage hunters with this lengthy process and it is best to begin your application for a hunting license well in advance of your trip.

When planning a hunting trip, write first to the Mexican Department of Wildlife, Dirección General de Flora y Fauna Silvestre, Nezahualcóyotl 109, 1er piso, Mexico DF 06080 for information and a hunting calendar which you can request printed in English. They should be able to help you with a special permit (which you need for certain species). You can also obtain information on permits from your nearest Mexican consulate and they will provide you with a hunting license on receipt of a tourist card, two passport-size photographs and a letter from your local police department vouching for your character. You must state which firearms you intend to take with you, where you intend to hunt and when. Before finalizing your plans, it's best to contact Mexican and United States customs who will be able to tell you the exact current regulations on the movement of guns from one country to another and what you may bring home with you from Mexico.

Tourist offices should be able to provide you with information on hunting with a registered guide if this is your preference. Visitors should always ensure that their firearms are registered with the Mexican National Defense Ministry. Mexican consulates will help you to register.

Jai alai: jai alai, or *frontón* as it is called in Spain, is of Basque origin and is said to be the fastest game in the world. It is played most evenings in Mexico City at the *Frontón México* and it is also popular in Tijuana and many smaller towns and villages.

Sailing: most coastal and lakeside resorts have small yachts for hire. Acapulco, Cabo San Lucas (in Baja California), Cancún, Cozumel, Manzanillo, Mazatlán and Puerto Vallarta are the main seaside resorts with facilities. Lakeside centers with facilities include Avándaro (Valle de Bravo) and Tequesquitengo (near Cuernavaca). Inquire at your hotel or at the beaches and lakeside shores. Regattas are held in some resorts, mainly Acapulco, Cozumel, Ensenada, Manzanillo and Mazatlán. For information you can apply to Federación Méxicana de Vela, Balderas 36, Piso 13, México 1 DF.

Scuba and skin diving: Mexico is a paradise for enthusiasts of scuba and skin diving and offers some of the best spots in the world. The warm, clear waters of the Caribbean abound in hundreds of varieties of tropical fish and magnificent coral formations. Notable places to visit are the Palancar Reef (off Isla Cozumel) which is the longest reef of its kind in the world; the pretty little lagoon of Chancanab also at Cozumel; El Garrafón at Isla Mujeres with its unique undersea coral garden; the Xel-Ha lagoons full of exotic fish, on the road to Tulum in Quintana Roo.

All major resorts down the Pacific coast are good for diving, including the eastern shores of Baja California. Main beach resorts have equipment for hire and can offer diving instruction, as well as organized diving tours.

Soccer: *fútbol*, is a very popular sport in Mexico. Games are played throughout the year at the magnificent Aztec Stadium, to the south of Mexico City. The stadium has a capacity for more than 100,000 fans and it is an important venue for the World Cup matches in 1970 and 1986. Major towns have stadiums and the most important are in Guadalajara, Puebla and León. Information regarding international matches can be obtained from the national football association either of Mexico or of the visiting country.

Spas: there are numerous warm water springs, known as *balnearios*, in Mexico and a few have been developed into attractive spa resorts. Most are located in the central regions of the country. Among the most popular spas with thermal pools, lovely accommodations and recreational activities are: Ixtapán de la Sal (state of México), San José Purúa (Michoacán), Oaxtepec Vacation Center (Morelos), Spa Peñafiel (Puebla) and Balneario Comanjilla (Guanajuato). Spas have been used for their healing and relaxing properties since before the Spanish conquest. Montezuma, the Aztec ruler, enjoyed the spa at the Oaxtepec Vacation Center. Your travel agent should be able to supply you with information on each of the popular spa resorts.

Surfing: Mexico has many magnificent beaches for surfing but the sport is still fairly new and there are only a few facilities at present. Some establishments which do rent surfboards may not always be reputable. Ideal conditions are to be found mainly along the immense stretch of coast down the Baja California peninsula and on the mainland Pacific coast, between Mazatlán and Puerto Escondido. Surfing is prohibited on crowded beaches but it is permitted in quiet areas. Surfers must check carefully for dangerous undercurrents and ask about the possibility of sharks in the area. It is also wise to look after your equipment carefully and guard against theft.

Swimming and sunbathing: except for its northern border with the United States and the southern borders with Guatemala and Belize, Mexico is surrounded by warm tropical waters and offers hundreds of miles of magnificent coastline and beaches. Some of Mexico's most popular and celebrated beach resorts are to be found along the Pacific coast, including Acapulco, Puerto Vallarta, Ixtapa/Zihuatanejo and Mazatlán. There are increasingly popular hotel developments stretching north of Manzanillo. With golden sands, palm trees, warm waters and a tropical climate, this area attracts thousands of visitors every year. Magnificent and often very quiet beaches are to be found along the Baja California coastline. The Caribbean coast includes such favorite island destinations as Cancún, Cozumel and Isla Mujeres. The powder-white beaches, shaded by palm trees, and warm, crystal-clear turquoise waters offer ideal conditions for swimming, although, at times, this region can be subject to certain changes of weather with sudden tropical storms. The beaches on the Gulf of Mexico are usually darker and conditions for swimming are less favorable with few real resorts.

Warm, tropical evenings and spectacular sunsets add to the attraction of beach holidays. Visitors should remember that the sun can be deceptively strong. Sunbathers should go carefully and take adequate precautions. If in doubt, ask your pharmacist to recommend a good, protective sun lotion.

Tennis: there are private tennis clubs in major cities such as Mexico City and Guadalajara. You will find more courts at resorts, particularly Acapulco, and many hotels have tennis courts for the use of their guests. Private clubs may permit visitors to play, provided they are invited as the guest of a member. For a list of clubs open to non-members, write to Federación Mexicana de Tenis, Durango 225-301, México D.F., Mexico. If you do play at a private tennis club, remember that facilities will be in greatest demand at weekends.

Walking and climbing: there are numerous remote and lovely areas in which to enjoy a good hike if you are familiar with the terrain, or accompanied by someone from the area. If you do not know the area, it would be wisest to take advantage of some of the National Parks which have marked trails for walks in magnificent surroundings. The following are particularly suitable: Desierto de los Leones, Nevada de Toluca (west of Mexico City), Lagunas de Zempoala (Morelos) and Cumbres de Ajusco (south of Mexico City), Lagunas de Montebello (Chiapas), San Pedro Mártir (Baja California norte) and Constitución de 1857 park at Rumorosa (Baja California norte).

Water skiing: equipment is available for hire at most popular coastal and lake resorts. Enquire locally.

Windsurfing: an increasingly popular sport in some resorts. Cozumel and Cancún, in particular, offer ideal conditions.

ENTERTAINMENT

Music and dancing have always played an integral role in the life of the Mexican. Almost every day of the year there is a fiesta or celebration in some part of the country where music plays an important part. (See introductions to regional sections for main fiestas in the region, and 'Fiestas', p. 26, for details of major festivals in the country). Music has deep roots in both Indian and Spanish cultures. In ancient times music and dance formed part of Indian religious ceremonies. The Aztecs played percussion and wind instruments while performing their rituals. After the conquest, the Spaniards introduced new musical forms and the guitar soon became a popular instrument. Each region has its own particular style of music, combining different instruments with varying tempos.

Perhaps the best known Mexican musical form is the performance of *mariachi* music. The name, *mariachi* is a derivation of the French word *mariage* meaning marriage. It was initially applied to musicians who played at weddings during the French occupation in the latter part of the 19th century. With their sombreros and silver studded costumes, the mariachis can be hired in groups to sing at special occasions and Mexican men hire *mariachis* to serenade their loves during the very early hours of the morning. You will find *mariachis* in the zócalos of most towns and no visitor should miss the chance to hear their music.

You will find many variations in music as you travel the country: *Jarocho* music from Veracruz is particularly lively. Musicians with striking red neckerchiefs sing and play the guitar and harp. Melancholy songs are played on the marimba by musicians in Oaxaca.

From the northern regions another type of sound has emerged — the lively *norteña* music. Accordions accompany stringed instruments and costumes bear resemblance to cowboy outfits, showing a marked influence from the United States.

More regular sophisticated forms of entertainment are to be found mainly in Mexico City, Guadalajara and Acapulco. Both Mexico City and Guadalajara have symphony orchestras which perform regularly and go on tour. Foreign orchestras and soloists often perform in Mexico's concert halls. Classical ballet and opera companies, both national and international, appear regularly in the larger cities. In Mexico City there are several outstanding buildings in which to enjoy Mexican music and ballet such as The Palacio de Bellas Artes (Palace of Fine Arts). Symphony concerts, opera and ballet performances are held at Guadalajara's Teatro Degollado at the Convention Center in Acapulco, and at theaters in Guanajuato, Oaxaca, Puebla and San Miguel de Allende.

Cities, towns and villages throughout Mexico feature open-air band concerts in parks and main squares all the year round. The world famous Ballet Folklórico, a dazzling presentation of Mexican folk music and dance from the various regions, is performed on Wednesdays and Sundays at the Palace of Fine Arts in Mexico City. Many hotels in larger cities and in resorts have restaurants and bars which offer musical entertainment and stay open until the early hours of the morning. A number of these also have a weekly 'Mexican Fiesta' with regional songs, dancing and a buffet of Mexican food. The best nightclubs and discotheques are usually to be found at luxury hotels and these are plentiful in major cities and resorts. Much of Mexico's pop music is imported from the United States and is played at discotheques.

Most plays in the Mexican theater are, of course, in Spanish but members of the United States community do sometimes give amateur performances in English.

There is always a good choice of films showing in Mexico City and if the films are foreign, they are shown in their original language, with Spanish sub-titles. Programs of films and other activities can be found in the English-language newspaper, the *News*. In resorts, a free information sheet is circulated at hotels, furnishing you with information on current events in the area. When information is available in advance, Mexican tourist offices or travel agents can probably provide you with details of major events. Details of local activities in areas which are less frequented by tourists are best obtained on the spot.

FIESTAS

Every town and village in Mexico holds one, or several, annual fiestas. Of the numerous festivals which take place, these can be considered among the most colorful and interesting:

Feb or Mar — *Carnival Week*. This starts a week before Ash Wednesday, with processions, floats, fireworks, regional songs, dances and cultural events. The celebrations take place in many parts of Mexico but the most famous are at Mazatlán (Sinaloa) and Veracruz (Veracruz).

Mar or Apr — Holy Week. Just before Easter, there are celebrations throughout the country. The Passion plays are of particular interest and you can watch notable versions in towns such as Taxco, Pátzcuaro and San Cristóbal de las Casas.

Apr 20 — May 1, *Feria de San Marcos* (San Marcos Fair). One of Mexico's liveliest festivals with dancing and bullfighting, Aguascalientes (Aguascalientes).

May or June — Corpus Christi Day. The ceremony of Los Voladores de Papantla (the flying men of Papantla) shouldn't be missed. Costumed dancers twirl down a tall pole by means of a rope which unties, leaving them free to 'fly' around the pole in circles with arms extended. This is done to the accompaniment of a haunting melody played by a flutist. The ceremony was performed in pre-conquest times as an ancient pagan rite. Papantla (Veracruz).

July 16-18 — Guelaguetza festival. Lunes del Cerro (Monday on the Hill). Indian groups from Oaxaca region gather and perform native dances, staged on the Cerro del Fortín (hill of the small fort). Very colorful. Just outside Oaxaca.

Sep 15, 16 — Independence Day. Celebrated throughout Mexico. On the night of the 15th the *Grito* is given: a re-enactment of the rallying cry by Father Hidalgo at the outbreak of the struggle for Independence from Spanish rule in 1810. In most places, excellent firework displays follow. On the 16th, there are grand processions, military parades, charros on horseback and lovely señoritas in beautiful costumes. Celebrations in Mexico City and Dolores Hidalgo (Guanajuato), where the Independence War began, are particularly boisterous.

Possibly Sep or Oct. Dates not yet determined. Cervantes Festival (Festival Cervantino). Now an International event, of about two weeks duration, with cultural events, theater, opera and concerts. Many nations participate in the festival. Guanajuato (Guanajuato).

Throughout Oct — *Fiestas de octubre.* Colorful festival in Guadalajara which takes place during the month of October. Daily events include concerts, art exhibitions, serenades, fireworks, cultural and sporting events. Guadalajara (Jalisco).

Nov 1, 2. Day of the Dead *Día de los Muertos* (Day of the Dead). Celebrated throughout the country but unique on the island of Janitzio on lake Pátzcuaro. The villagers bring offerings of flowers and food to the gravesides of their loved ones and hold an all-night wake (Michoacán).

Dec 12 — fiesta of Our Lady of Guadalupe, the patroness of Mexico. Songs and dances from all over the country are performed in front of the shrine. Mexicans make pilgrimages to the shrine in almost unending processions around this time.

Dec 16-24 — Christmas festivities. Every night at this time of year, families and neighbors get together to re-enact in song and verse the search for shelter at the *posada* (inn), carrying lighted candles and images of Joseph and Mary. A festive party then follows. There are magnificent illuminations in Mexico City from early December.

Mexican Tourist offices should be able to advise you regarding dates and timings

Night of the Dead ceremony — an important Mexican holiday

of fiestas but remember that Mexicans have a reputation for poor time keeping and dates change quite frequently. Most fiestas will take place on the dates given by your hotel or travel agent but in Mexico you should not always expect fiestas to commence exactly according to timings and it is best to be flexible.

WHAT YOU NEED TO KNOW

Antiquities: no authentic archaeological pieces, Spanish colonial art, or original artifacts, may be taken out of the country. Not only will the items be confiscated, but a fine or even imprisonment may be imposed. There is also a restriction on the export of gold and silver coins. If interested in any of these items you should contact the Mexican customs authorities.

Churches: Mexico is predominantly a Catholic country and every town and village has its church. The church makes no rules on clothing but, as a courtesy, it should be dignified and discreet. There are services in English at some of the churches in larger cities and resorts such as Mexico City, Guadalajara, Monterrey, Cuernavaca and Acapulco. Synagogues and Protestant churches can be found in major centers. Check with your hotel, local tourist office or Mexican consulate. The English language *News* prints times of services.

Cigarettes and tobacco: Mexican brands are plentiful and cheap. United States brands are sold in Mexico but it is not usually possible to obtain British brands.

Electricity: Mexico now operates the United States system of 60-cycle 110-117 volt AC with flat 2-pin sockets, and United States citizen's electrical appliances such as shavers and hair dryers will operate normally but the current may be weaker in remoter areas. Travelers from the United Kingdom will need an adaptor to fit the flat 2-pin sockets and these should be bought beforehand.

Health: no inoculations are required when you visit Mexico unless you have recently visited an infected area. (See 'Travel Documents', p. 12 for advice on health insurance.) Two main hazards to watch out for are stomach upsets, commonly known as 'Montezuma's Revenge', and sunburn. The first complaint can be caused by a number of things. The best way to minimize the risk is to avoid changing your habits too quickly. Give your body time to adjust to the different eating times, types of food and altitudes. For example alcohol will have a much greater effect on you at higher altitudes than it does at home. It is wise to avoid drinking tap water and drinks with ice in them. Use purification tablets or buy bottled water and remember to peel fruit and wash it in purified water. Try to avoid uncooked vegetables and unpasteurised, uncooked dairy products. In top international hotels, the water should be of the same high standard as you would expect at home.

Medicines and tablets are readily available in Mexico, but to be sure that the pharmacist's remedy doesn't cause any problems, it is best to bring your own firstaid kit. Before leaving home, visitors should consult a doctor or pharmacist for information on which medicines to bring.

Sunbathers are not always aware of the strength of the sun's rays and it is best to consult your pharmacist on the most effective protective lotions available.

If you require the services of a doctor or dentist in Mexico, hotel desk clerks are usually helpful. If you provide your home address when checking in, the hotel will be able to inform your national consulate if you fall ill. You can also consult the yellow pages of the telephone directory for a *médico* (doctor) or a *dentista* (dentist). Medical services are good but they are provided for a fee. Alternatively, in the case of an accident, you can receive free emergency help from the Mexican Red Cross (557 5758). Citizens of the United Kingdom should be aware that there is no reciprocal national health agreement with Mexico and it is wise to take out insurance before departure.

The American–British Cowdray Hospital (known as the ABC Hospital or the Hospital Inglés) is located on Calle Sur e Observatorio, Mexico 18, D.F. The hospital has an intensive care unit and emergency services. To reach the switchboard, dial 277 5000 and for emergencies, dial 515 8359; Outside Mexico City, ask at your hotel or look under *hospitals* and *sanatorios* in the telephone directory.

Lost property: there is no official office to deal with this situation but if you lose any belongings while traveling, report this immediately upon arrival at your destination. Any other losses should be reported to the police or your consulate. For advice on travel insurance, see 'Travel Documents' p. 12.

Mail: every sizeable town or village in Mexico has a post office, known as a *casa de correos*. Mail boxes, known as *buzones*, are to be found in post offices, outside some large public buildings and in major hotels. You can buy stamps in post offices, hotels and some stores which sell postcards. Post offices are usually open from 9 am until 7 pm Monday to Friday and 9 am to 5 pm on Saturdays. Some close for a while in the early afternoon. You can arrange for mail (marked 'tourist mail') to be sent to you at your hotel. Main post offices will also hold mail for you if it is addressed to you a/c Lista de Correos (care of delivery). Proof of identity is required before you can pick up any mail. American Express will hold mail for their customers at local offices. (see 'Useful addresses', p. 31 for the Mexico City branch.) If you are sending letters within the country or abroad, keep the name and address simple and clear. If you use airmail, your letters will reach their destination much more quickly. Parcels should be registered to ensure their delivery.

Newspapers and magazines: a number of publications in the English language are available in Mexico. One of the most useful is the *News* — a daily newspaper with worldwide news and features sold throughout Mexico.

The *Daily Bulletin* offers short news bulletins and some tourist information. It is distributed to hotels, news stands and some restaurants in Mexico City. *Amistad* is a monthly publication for Americans living in Mexico. It can be purchased from the editorial offices at Río Pánuco 15, Mexico City. Foreign newspapers, especially from the United States, are available at Sanborn stores, some news stands and at hotels. A number of free publications aimed at tourists give information on events and attractions. They are available in hotels, and some shops. Names to look out for include 'Guide', 'This Week', 'The Gazer' and 'Now in Mexico'.

Opening times: offices, stores and public buildings have different opening and closing times and these can vary from one city to another. Some close for a period during the day while others stay open all day. Stores generally stay open all day, from about 9 or 10 am until 7 or 8 pm. In popular resorts some shops stay open later. Sunday opening is optional. Banks are generally open Monday to Friday from 9 am to 1.30 pm. The main offices of some banks are open on Saturday mornings and a few have been experimenting with Sunday mornings, but do not count on finding one open at weekends. Drugstores are usually open all day throughout the week and a few are open late at night. Enquire at your hotel. Offices and businesses usually work a 5 or 6 day week. Many close in the early afternoon, often from 2 until 4 pm. Some may even close until 6 pm.

Museum opening hours vary and most close one day each week. Some close for a period in the early afternoon and some stay open later one day during the week. Restaurants and bars stay open late as many people only begin their meal around 10 pm. Many coffee shops and chain restaurants are open day and night. Banks, stores and offices close on National Holidays and sometimes the day before and after.

Photography: each traveler into Mexico is permitted to bring one still camera, one portable movie camera and 12 rolls of film for each. Film is readily available in Mexico but as it can be expensive and may not always be of the best quality, it is a good idea to bring your film with you. In some museums you will be expected to buy a separate ticket to photograph exhibits. It is illegal to take photographs of military installations. Photographing local Indians can be difficult as they often look upon the camera as a form of witchcraft and you should ask their consent first. Some of the scenery in Mexico is breathtaking and there are excellent opportunities to take good photographs.

Police: the uniform varies throughout the country but in Mexico City, traffic and civil police have pale blue uniforms. Different uniforms are worn by parking police, bank guards and others. Some of the police on patrol in certain tourist areas are bilingual and can offer helpful advice to visitors. If, for any reason, you are stopped by the police, be polite and try to be helpful.

Public holidays: government and private offices, stores, post offices and banks close on public holidays and sometimes on the days preceding and following; Jan 1, New Year's Day (Año Nuevo); Feb 5, Constitution Day; Mar 21, birthday of Benito Juárez; Mar/Apr, Holy Thursday and Good Friday; May 1, Labor Day. May 5, anniversary of defeat of the French in the Battle of Puebla in 1862; Sept 1, President's state-of-the-Union Report and opening of Congress; Sept 16, Independence Day; Oct 12, Columbus Day; (Día de la Raza); Nov 1, 2, Day of the Dead; Nov 20, anniversary of the Mexican Revolution of 1910; Dec 12, Day of our Lady of Guadalupe (Día de Nuestra Señora de Guadalupe); Dec 25, Christmas Day.

Shopping: Mexico has an enormous variety of colorful goods produced from different regions all over the country. Part of the fun of shopping is browsing around, particularly in local markets, where haggling with the vendors is expected. Although it helps if you speak some Spanish, English is usually understood in tourist areas. Towns and villages have daily or weekly markets and a visit is certainly recommended. It is usually cheaper to buy goods in the areas where they are produced and you may have the chance of watching the craftsmen at work. You can often pick up a bargain but watch out for poorly made goods.

Shops in tourist centers usually stay open late. In these shops, you pay the price asked for and visitors are not expected to try to bargain with the salesman. You can find almost anything in Mexico City and FONART, the Government-run chain of stores, sells a wide selection of regional handicrafts and jewelry. Silver is a specialty of Mexico. The main center is the picturesque little town of Taxco, where there are countless shops offering beautiful silverware and jewelry. The standard of design and workmanship is high, but check the hallmark for the top quality items. Prices are not necessarily lower here, however, than elsewhere in Mexico. Mexico produces a number of semi-precious stones which can be bought loose or set tastefully in silver (or sometimes in gold) in the form of rings, bracelets and necklaces. Prices should be reasonable. Beware of paying a high price unless you are sure that the value of the stone is as indicated.

Among many other beautiful items produced in the country, the following are suggestions for popular buys (but remember you will have to travel home and through customs with your purchases): ceramics; pottery; glassware; artifacts of onyx (ashtrays, boxes, carved figures, chess sets and coffee tables); colorful woven and embroidered goods; leather goods from Yucatán; papier maché figures; exquisite candles in all shapes and colors; innumerable decorative items for the home in materials such as copper, brass, the turquoise malachite stone. This is an ideal country for finding attractive and unusual gifts to bring home. *Amates*, which are colorful bark paintings, are very suitable, and light-weight; tasteful and well-made reproductions of pre-Columbian artifacts are also a good buy but beware of cheap copies. For men's casual wear in resorts, the *guayabera* pin-tucked shirt from the Yucatán can be bought in most shops and is cool and comfortable. You can buy attractive and elegant attire, often reasonably priced, in the major resorts. It is normally cheaper to buy Mexican goods rather than those which have been imported.

Telephones and telegrams: in all cities there are public telephone booths where local calls can be made by inserting a coin, and dialling. Try to carry a few coins with you at all times for this eventuality. For long distance calls from a public booth it is best to call the operator — dial 02 — and ask for a collect call, *por cobrar*.

International operators — dial 09 — usually speak English. Major towns have special long distance call offices (Cabina de larga distancia). It is much cheaper to call from here than from your hotel but you may have to spend a long time waiting for other people to finish. It is simpler to make a long distance call from your hotel but there is quite a high surcharge. If you are using a pay phone, remember to press the button which releases your coin into the phone box.

International and domestic telegrams are most easily sent from your hotel desk or they may also be transmitted through the central telegraph office in Mexico City at Balderas 14, Mexico 1, D.F. It is not possible to transfer charges. Domestic telegrams are cheap and reliable. International telegrams are more expensive. Three classes of service may be used for international telegrams, 'straight wire, day letter and night letter.

Time differentials: most areas in Mexico are on the central standard time (6 hours behind GMT). The north-western states of Nayarit, Sinaloa, Sonora and Baja California Sur, operate on mountain time (7 hours behind GMT) and Baja California norte is on Pacific standard time (8 hours behind GMT). Baja California norte is the only state which observes daylight savings. Local time is usally announced by the airline captain just before landing and do remember to adjust your watch accordingly. The 24-hour clock is used for timetables in Mexico with midnight referred to as 2400 and 6 pm as 1800.

Tipping: many Mexicans who work in the service industries in particular receive a very low wage and they rely upon tips for their livelihood. It is customary to leave a tip, however small, in many situations where you would perhaps not do so back home. The amount you may wish to give will, of course, depend upon the particular service performed but, the amount you normally give at home is usually a good guide. Service is rarely included in hotel and restaurant bills and 15% of the bill is the usual tip. Any other tips left in the hotel should be offered directly to a particular member of the staff who has given you special service. It is customary to leave a gratuity in your room upon your departure for the chamber maids. The following tipping guidelines are included only as suggestions:

no tip expected — taxi drivers
5 pesos — minimum tip
5-10 pesos — gas station attendants
10-20 pesos — parking attendants and/or car watchers per hour
50-100 pesos — bellboys, porters

10-15% of the bill — hair salons, waiters. Always try to have some coins with you for unexpected situations which can arise. Tips should rise with inflation.

Toilets: apart from airports and railway stations there are few public toilets. It is best to avoid them and seek the nearest hotel or restaurant if necessary, although standards of hygiene can leave much to be desired even in some of the smarter establishments. It is a good idea to carry tissues and soap as you will often find they are missing. You are not expected to leave a tip. Men's washrooms are signposted as *hombres, caballeros* or *señores* and ladies rooms are labelled *damas, mujeres* or *señoras*.

USEFUL ADDRESSES

Mexican consulates will help you to obtain information and issue you with official papers. There are Mexican consulates and honorary consulates in most major United States cities. Check with your directory. In the United Kingdom the Mexican consulate is at 8 Halkin St, London SW1. In Canada there are Mexican consulates at the following addresses: 1000 Sherbrooke W., Suite 2170, Montreal; Mexican Embassy, 130 Albert St, Room 206, Ottawa, K1P 5G4; Commerce Court East, Suite 1310, P.O. Box 255, Toronto M5L 1E9; 625 Howe St, Suite 310, V6C 2T6; 1808 Kensington Building, 275 Portage Ave, P.O. Box 1648.

Consulates in Mexico

British, United States and Canadian consulates will provide their nationals with helpful information in an emergency.

There are consul generals maintained by the United States in the following Mexican cities: Mexico City (United States Embassy, Paseo de la Reforma 305, Mexico 06500 D.F.), Ciudad Juárez, Guadalajara, Hermosillo, Matamoros, Mazatlán, Mérida, Monterrey, Mexico City, Nuevo Laredo, Tijuana. There are also consular agents in Acapulco, Cancún, Durango, Oaxaca, Puerto Vallarta, San Luis Potosí, Tampico, Tuxtla Gutiérrez and Veracruz.

Embassy of Great Britain: Río Lerma 71, México 5, D.F. The consulate is at Usamacinta 30, Col. Cuauhtémoc, México 06500, México D.F. Consuls and vice consuls are maintained in Acapulco and other main cities.

Canadian Embassy: Schiller 529, Mexico 11570, D.F.

Australian Embassy, Paseo de la Reforma 195, 5th floor, Mexico 16500, Mexico D.F.

Visa matters for New Zealand citizens are handled by the British Embassy.

Other useful addresses: AMA *(Asociación Mexicana Automovilística)* Orizaba 7, Mexico, D.F., Mexico 06700. There are branches in Mexico City, Guadalajara, Veracruz, Puebla, Jalapa and Chihuahua and the organization is affiliated to the American Automobile Association.

American Express Travel Service, Hamburgo 75, Mexico 6, D.F.

Central Post Office *(Oficina de Correos)*, Correo Mayor, Tacuba y Ruiz Alarcon, Mexico 1, D.F.

International Telegrams, Balderas 14, Mexico 1, D.F.

Secretaría de Turismo, Mariano Escobedo 726, Mexico, D.F. All major cities and tourist centers have a government tourist office of information, often located in the town hall. Your hotel will be able to direct you to it.

American-British Cowdray Hospital, Calle Sur e Observatorio, Mexico 18, D.F. switchboard no. 277 5000. Emergency 515 8359.

Useful telephone numbers: police 06; ambulance, Red Cross *(Cruz Roja)* 557 5758/9/60; Tourist information for Mexico City 250 0123.

Mexican Tourist Offices abroad:

United States

10100 Santa Monica Boulevard, Los Angeles, CA 90067; 405 Park Avenue, Suite 1001, New York, N.Y. 10022; 100 North Biscayne Blvd., Suite 2804, Miami, Fla 33132; Cain Tower, 229 Peachtree St., Suite 1201, Atlanta, GA 30303; Two Illinois Center, 233 North Michigan Ave., Suite 1413, Chicago, Il. 60601; 2707 North Loop West, Suite 450, Houston, Tx. 77008.

Canada:

One Place Ville Marie, Suite 2409, Montreal, Quebec H3B 3M9; PO Box 49323, Four Bentall Center Suite 2754, 1055 Dunsmuir Street, Vancouver, B.C. V7X 1L4; 181 University Avenue, Suite 1112, Toronto, Ontario, CA. M5H 3M7.

United Kingdom

7 Cork St., London W1X 1PB.

THE LANGUAGE

Spanish is the language of Mexico, although there are still a great number of ancient Indian languages spoken in different parts of the country. There are certain differences between the Spanish spoken in Mexico and that of Spain. The Mexican pronunciation is softer, the intonation more drawn out and the language is richer and more flexible. Mexicans and Span-

iards have no difficulty in understanding each other but the accent and different words and expressions used in each of these countries can immediately pinpoint the nationality. Once you have listened for a while, you realise that Spanish is a phonetic language which is fairly logical to pronounce and spell.

Notes on pronunciation: in Mexico there is no 'lisping' sound on the **z** as there is in Spain. Letters **c** and **z** before 'e' or 'i' are pronounced like an 's'.

Many old Indian names have an **'x'** in them and the pronunciation can vary. It can sound like an 'h' (eg Oaxaca is pronounced wah-hah-kah) but it can also sound like 'z' as in Xochimilco (zo-chee-meel-co). For names like Ixtapa, pronounce the 'x' as 'sh' as in 'dish' (Ishtah-pah). If a letter has an accent marked over it, the letter should be pronounced with greater stress.

g (before 'e' or 'i') — sounds like an 'h' eg hide.

g (before 'a', 'o' or 'u') — sounds like hard 'g' eg gate, hug.

j — sounds like 'h' eg hall, hide.

double l — sounds like 'y' eg yoyo.

q (followed by 'u') — sounds like 'k' eg duck.

ñ — sounds like 'ny' eg canyon.

English is quite widely spoken in major towns and tourist centers, but most Mexicans very much appreciate any visitor who tries to speak even a few words in Spanish, however limited his vocabulary. They regard this as a courtesy towards their country and they will usually show patience and understanding with your efforts. The simplest of phrases will always create good will. If you are planning to travel in more remote areas, it is best to have at least some basic grasp of the language.

Travelers to Mexico should purchase a good Spanish phrase book, such as *Collins Spanish Phrase Book*, but a brief list of useful words and phrases is given below:

Good morning   *Buenos días*
Good afternoon/evening   *Buenas tardes*
Good night   *Buenas noches*
Many thanks   *Muchas gracias*
Not at all/you're welcome   *de nada*
Pleased to meet you   *Mucho gusto*
How are you?   *como está usted?*
Very well thank you   *Muy bien, gracias*
What is your name?   *Cual es su nombre?*
I don't understand   *no entiendo*
I don't speak Spanish   *no hablo español*
Do you speak English   *habla usted inglés?*
Do you understand me?   *me comprende?*
Excuse me   *perdón*
yes   *si*
no   *no*
please   *por favor*

Where is . . .   *dónde está . . . ?*
How long?   *Cuánto tiempo?*
When   *Cuándo?*
What time is it?   *Qué hora es?*
Can you please help me?   *Puede usted ayudarme por favor?*
How much is?   *Cuánto es?*
I would like   *quisiera*
Keep the change   *Quedese con el cambio*
Where is the ladies' room?   *Dónde está el baño de damas?*
Where is the men's room?   *Dondé está el baño de caballeros?*
Where is the phone?   *Dónde está el teléfono?*

airport   *aeropuerto*
afternoon   *tarde*
archaeological site   *zona arqueológica*
art gallery   *museo de arte*
bay   *bahía*
beach   *playa*
border   *frontera*
bus stop   *parada de autobus*
cathedral   *catedral*
castle   *castillo*
chapel   *capilla*
church   *iglesia*
cold   *frío*
dentist   *dentista*
doctor   *médico*
fountain   *fuente*
gas station   *gasolinera*
guide   *guía*
men   *señores, hombres, caballeros*
harbor or port   *puerto*
hospital   *hospital*
hot   *caliente*
house   *casa*
ladies   *señoras, damas, mujeres*
market   *mercado*
morning   *mañana*
museum   *museo*
new   *ahora*
park   *parque*
pharmacist (all night)   *farmacia (de guardia)*
post office   *correo*
pyramid   *pirámide*
railway station   *la estación del ferrocarril*
spa   *balneario*
stadium   *estadio*
street   *calle*
temple   *templo*
theater   *teatro*
tourist office   *oficina de turismo*
tower   *torre*

MEXICO CITY

Mexico City is one of the highest cities in the world. It lies in the Valley of Mexico at an altitude of 7350 ft (2250 m), surrounded by a ring of mountains rising a further 3000 ft (920 m). As you fly over it by day, the first sight of this gigantic, sprawling metropolis can be impressive. To approach it by night is even more memorable. From the engulfing darkness below the glittering lights of the city unfold in the distance and suddenly, as you pass over it, the whole area becomes a sparkling patchwork of lights.

Mexico City, which is referred to by the Mexicans simply as 'Mexico', is the seat of government and the political, economic and cultural center of the country. It spreads over a good proportion of the Valley and is growing annually at an alarming rate, with the daily influx of people from the provinces creating increasing social and economic problems. Its population in 1985 is estimated to have reached more than 12 million and it is in the process of becoming the largest city in the world, already with a projected population of 25 million by the year 2000.

Mexico City is the oldest city in the Western Hemisphere. It was built by the Spanish Conquistadores on the ruins of the mighty ancient Aztec capital, Tenochtitlán. Tenochtitlán dates back to around the middle of the 14th century. Many thousands of years ago, when the first known Indian groups arrived in the Valley of Mexico (Valle de Anáhuac) the area was a mass of lakes and little islands and porous land. Villages appeared around the shores of the lakes and the Indians began cultivating corn and developing an agricultural way of life. The Aztecs arrived in the Central Highlands towards the end of the 13th century and wandered about the valley seeking a site on which to settle. When they came upon an eagle perched on a cactus and swallowing a snake, they took this as a sign from the god of war, Huitxilopochtli, of the fulfilment of a prophecy and built their city on that spot in the middle of the great lake Texcoco. They constructed causeways leading to the mainland and on the site where the eagle had appeared, the Aztecs erected a temple which they called the Halls of Montezuma. It is now the main square of the city, known as the zócalo.

During the folllowing 200 years the Aztecs conquered many neighboring tribes and created an Empire which spread far over the surrounding areas. The city, Tenochtitlán, grew into a metropolis of an estimated 300,000 inhabitants, far larger than European cities of the time, with an immense main marketplace square and several magnificent palaces and temples, dominated by the Great Temple.

A mariachi plays to celebrate a local fiesta

Mexico City

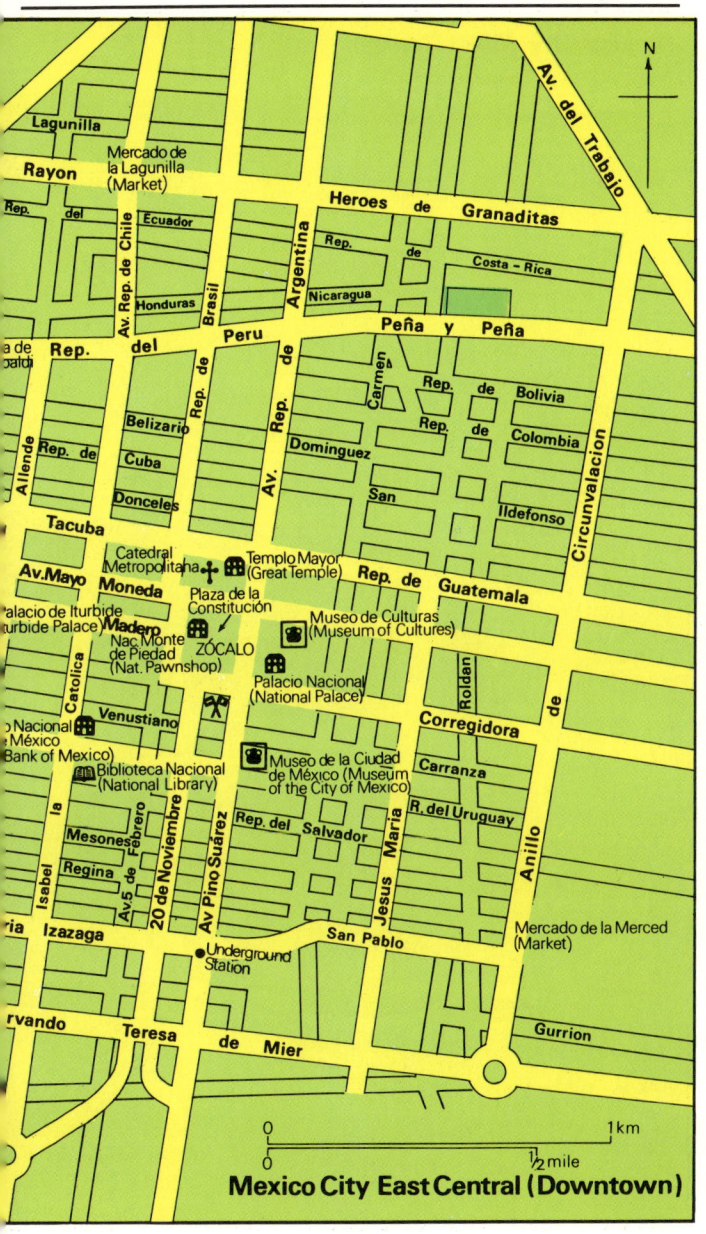

40   Mexico City

The zócalo at night

Mexico City

In 1519 Hernán Cortés and his band of followers arrived in Veracruz and set forth on their historic march to the great Aztec capital. When they first set eyes on this vast city shimmering on the lake they were utterly amazed by its sheer size and grandeur and dazzled by its brilliant color. At the culmination of the two year struggle which ensued between the Aztecs and the Spaniards, the city was almost totally destroyed and little now remains of the ancient capital. The Spanish built a new city on the old site and this became the capital of New Spain. Some fine buildings, such as the National Palace, the Cathedral and several others were constructed on the old foundations in the zócalo. The Spanish gained considerable wealth during their 300 year rule from the prosperous gold and silver mining industries and such wealth was evident in the capital. The famous explorer and traveler Baron Alexander von Humboldt, visited Mexico City during his travels in the 18th century and referred to it as the City of Palaces. Compared to modern Mexico City, however, it remained a comparatively small town until the early 20th century when it began to expand and spread out in all directions over the valley. Highrise buildings, banks and hotels appeared and the Mexico City of today has some of the most exciting modern architecture to be seen anywhere. The **Plaza de las Tres Culturas** (Plaza of the Three Cultures) in the Tlatelolco district of the city's northern area displays buildings from the three eras of Mexico's history standing side by side. Here you can see the ruins of a pyramid (marking the spot where the Aztecs were finally defeated by Cortés), the Spanish colonial church of Santiago and the Convent of the Cross, and the tall modern building of the Secretaría de Relaciones Exteriores (Secretariat Building of Foreign Relations), which was completed just a few years ago. Three cultures stand side by side, the ancient, the old and the modern.

Mexico City is a natural gateway from which to start your journey to other parts of Mexico and you should certainly make a point of spending some time exploring this fascinating and complex city, with its blend of old and new cultures. When you arrive, remember that you are over 7000 ft (2000 m) above sea level and the air is thinner. It is advisable to take things easy for the first day or so until you become accustomed to the altitude. The climate is mild and varies little over the year, with an average temperature of 55°F in December and 63°F in June. Daytime is usually pleasantly warm, whereas it can be cool in the early morning and at night in the winter months. You can get lovely clear, sunny days, others can be obstructed by one of Mexico City's problems, smog, which all too often hovers over the city like a grey cloud. There is not much rain during the winter and usually a little each day between May and October.

The city is full of vitality, bursting with life, noise and color. The merging of the ancient Indian and Hispanic cultures in the 16th century has produced a unique combination which adds to modern Mexico's character. This is a city of extraordinary contrasts, where traces of its eventful and often turbulent past are evident everywhere and tall, modern office blocks, skyscrapers and hotels line the elegant tree-lined Paseo de la Reforma, exhibiting the lifestyle of 20th century Mexico.

Green parks, lovely fountains and brilliantly-colored flower markets grace the city. In the old but lively part of the city (downtown) there are houses and churches which date back to the colonial era and in the narrow streets you can buy from Indians selling their wares. You will pass stalls crammed with sweets and snacks, newspaper kiosks, shoeshine stands and vendors selling all sorts of things from balloons to lottery tickets. There is the continuous trill of the traffic policeman's whistle as he directs the swell of traffic through town. Sleek expensive cars glide alongside ramshackle old vehicles and there are traffic jams at certain times of the day.

Transport

Mexico City is not particularly suitable for sightseeing on foot. Distances are enormous and to maneuver yourself across some of the wider avenues, especially at the intersections, takes some doing! As the sidewalk is quite high above the street and often in need of repair, you should watch your step carefully. There are some pleasant areas, however, where you can enjoy a stroll. The Zona Rosa (Pink Zone) has many shops, boutiques, restaurants and some sidewalk cafés. The downtown area has some fascinating shops in which to browse around, markets and interesting old buildings. This area, in particular, is full of people and you are advised to take good care of your handbag or wallet. On a sunny day it is also very pleasant to take a leisurely stroll along parts of the lovely Paseo de la Reforma boulevard. It is not advisable to walk around town at night. A good way to begin your visit to Mexico City is to take an organized sightseeing tour. Plenty are available and can be arranged easily through your hotel or with a travel agent in town. They usually cover an enormous amount in one day and are good value. This will give you a chance to acclimatize yourself and get your bearings while seeing some of the city's main attractions.

There are plenty of buses crossing the city but some are in a state of dilapidation, packed and pickpockets are often at work. There are some better lines which are comparatively comfortable and travel along the main boulevards. Fares are very cheap.

Mexico City's metro system is quiet and efficient and the cost of traveling is very cheap. When work started in 1967 hundreds of artifacts and relics from Aztec times were uncovered. While most of these were taken to various museums, some remains were left and in one of the stations, called Pino Suárez, visitors can admire the Aztec shrine to Ehecatl, god of wind. Piped music is played in the stations which are decorated in a colorful way and there are shops. During the rush hour periods, the trains get so packed that you may have to wait for several to go by until you can board.

One of the easiest ways of getting around is by taxi. Upon arrival at Mexico City airport you have the choice of taking a 'colectivo' or a private taxi. The 'colectivo' is a little mini van which fills up with a maximum of 6 people and, for a set price payable in advance, drops you off at any central point in town. This is the most economical way of traveling from the airport. Otherwise you can take any one of the cars lined up ready to take you into town. These are more expensive and the price should be agreed upon before setting off. There are several different types of taxi in the city. The *peseros* are the most economical. They cruise along the main avenues on set routes and cram in as many people as they can. They are usually painted white with a colored stripe, and the driver holds out his fingers as he drives along to indicate how many seats are left. The charge used to be one peso, regardless of distance (hence the name *pesero*). Now it has risen but it is still remarkably cheap. There are hundreds of metered Volkswagens teeming about the city and they are very cheap, but nearly always occupied and it can be difficult to get one. They are usually orange or yellow with white stripes. White *sitio* taxis with orange stripes can only be caught at a cabstand as they do not cruise around looking for passengers and they charge a set price which should be fixed before departure. *Turismo* are large cars with English-speaking drivers which can offer extra service and have a higher charge. At larger hotels there is usually a taxi stand in front of the hotel with different types of vehicles including *Turismo*-type transportation. The doorman will always help you get a taxi if required. Hotel taxis often charge a little more than other types but they do offer a good service. Beware of the large cabs which tout for business and approach you in the street. They are likely to charge a high price. Some cab drivers may try to overcharge. There is little you can do about this if the driver won't give way unless you wish to make a formal complaint to the tourist industry. You can leave a small tip in the case of metered taxis but drivers of unmetered vehicles expect none.

You can rent a car from any of the major international rental companies such as Hertz, Avis or Budget but bear in mind that traffic in Mexico City can be confusing for any newcomer and parking facilities are not always easy to find. Your home driving licence is accepted.

Mexico City's major attractions can be grouped into several areas and the independent traveler would do well to concentrate on one district at a time. The **zócalo** is the historical heart of the old part of the city, referred to as 'Downtown'; the **Zona Rosa** (Pink Zone) is the fashionable area for shops and elegant restaurants; **Chapultepec Park** contains the finest museums; in the south you can visit the floating gardens of **Xochimilco, University City**, whose buildings have striking murals and the pretty **San Ángel** district; to the north you can visit places of archaeological and historical interest such as the **Basilica of Guadalupe,** the **Plaza of the Three Cultures,** the magnificent pyramids at **Teotihuacán** and many more sites outside the city in the state of México.

Downtown

A good place to start is the old **Plaza de la Constitución,** known simply as the zócalo. Every town and village in Mexico has its zócalo which is the main square and is the focal point of the local community. Mexico City's zócalo covers a huge area, second in size only to the Red Square of Moscow. It occupies what was once the central market place of ancient Tenochtitlán and was the site of the Halls of Montezuma.

Important buildings surround the zócalo. The **Palacio Nacional** (National Palace) on the east side was built by Cortés on the rubble left from destroyed Aztec buildings and it became the official residence of the Spanish Viceroys during the colonial period. It was also used by Emperor Maximilian during his short term as Emperor of Mexico (1864-1867) and since then by all the Mexican Presidents. Today it houses offices of the Presi-

Mexico City

Independence monument 'El Angel'

The Latin American Tower from Alameda Park

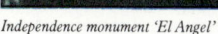
Palace of the Fine Arts

dent, the Finance Secretariat, the Benito Juárez museum and the National Archives. Its outstanding feature is its set of Diego Rivera murals and particularly those which adorn the main staircase. The bell said to have been the one used in the village of Dolores by Father Hidalgo to signal the start of the Independence Wars in 1810 hangs over the central portal. At 11 pm every year on 15 September, the President of Mexico rings this bell to start off the Independence Day celebrations.

The **Museo de las Culturas** (Museum of Cultures), on the street called Moneda behind the National Palace, was used as a mint during the period of Spanish rule and houses an interesting collection of artifacts from many parts of the world. On the northeast corner of the zócalo, you can visit the **Nacional Monte de Piedad** (National Pawnshop) which dates back to 1775. It is a fascinating place in which to spend some time browsing around. The **Templo Mayor** (Great Temple) on the northeast side of the cathedral was a sacred Aztec temple and there have recently been some excavations of great significance. Hundreds of artifacts, weapons, masks and statues were discovered here including an altar to the Aztec moon goddess, Coyolxauhqui. The **Catedral Metropolitana** (Metropolitan Cathedral), which stands on the north side of the zócalo, took 250 years to build and was completed in the late 18th century. It reflects several different styles of architecture and houses a fine collection of valuable works of art from the colonial period.

The **National Arts Museum** on Tacuba Street is an outstanding building with an excellent display of Mexican art from several eras. Lectures, courses and cultural activities take place here.

Leading from the zócalo, there are several old and narrow streets crammed with shops selling fine jewelry and silverware. The most prominent street in the area is Calle Madero leading westward from the zócalo. This old street which used to be known as the avenue of the silversmiths has some of Mexico's most distinguished shops. Buildings of historic interest in Calle Madero include the beautiful 18th century mansion called **Palacio de Iturbide** (Iturbide Palace) which was the home of Emperor Augustín de Iturbide during his short reign following Independence. The building now houses the Banco Nacional de México. The **Church of San Francisco** with its Churrigueresque façade is worth a visit. This was once part of a huge Franciscan monastery, most of which was destroyed in the 1860s. Across from here you can visit the **Casa de los Azulejos** (House of Tiles) which is an attractive building now housing a restaurant with a façade entirely covered by blue and white tiles. It is believed to have been built by the son of a Count of Valle de Orizaba. The Count was exasperated by his son's tendency to shirk work and told him that he would never prosper, saying 'You will never have a house of tiles'. The son then successfully set out to prove him wrong by becoming wealthy and covering the building with tiles.

The **Torre Latino Americana** (Latin American Tower) is a 44 story-high pillar of glass which is still a city landmark although its reputation as Mexico City's tallest building has now been taken over by the Pemex company's headquarters. On a clear day, the observations deck on top affords you a fantastic view of the city and mountains. Only a short distance away, you can visit the **Palacio de Bellas Artes** (Palace of Fine Arts) which is the home of the national opera and theater. There are ballet and Mexican folk performances on Wednesdays and Sundays. The luxurious building, which has an auditorium capable of seating 3500 people, was constructed in the early 20th century and took 34 years to complete. The Italian marble from which it was built is so heavy that the building has since begun to sink into the subsoil. The most striking feature is the famous Tiffany stained-glass curtain depicting the beautiful volcanoes, Popocatépetl and Ixtaccihuatl. From the balconies you can see murals by some of Mexico's most famous muralists.

Other attractions in the Downtown area include the **Museo de la Ciudad de México** (Museum of the City of Mexico) on the northeast corner of Pino Suárez. This is an 18th-century mansion where visitors can see a display showing the history of the city. The **Banco Nacional de México** (National Bank of Mexico), on the corner of Isabel Católica and Venustiano Carranza, is a lovely 17th-century house with a small art museum.

The pleasant, green **Alameda Park**, with its fountains and many trees, is dominated by a large statue of Mexico's famous President, Benito Juárez. The park is considered to be the central point of the city. The **Museo de Arte Popular** (Museum of Popular Art) on Avenida Juárez is a large government-controlled exbibition hall where you can buy crafts from all regions of Mexico.

The original Paseo de la Reforma, where it now crosses Avenida Juárez and travels westward to Chapultepec, was built according to the instructions of Emperor Maximilian who ordered that it should connect his residence at Chapultepec Park with the downtown area. The result was a boulevard probably as magnificent as the Champs Élysées in Paris. This elegant avenue is one of the most attractive features of the city, with palms and other varieties of trees lining the wide pavements and there is a pedestrian walking area if you feel like a stroll. The Reforma is flanked on either side by towering buildings housing banks, hotels, offices, Embassies, airline offices, cinemas and restaurants. At intervals the boulevard is broken by traffic circles known as *glorietas* which are crowned by monuments. There is a graceful statue to the **Angel of Independence,** referred to as 'El Angel' — a gilded figure on top of a tall column. This depicts the goddess of liberty, commemorating Mexico's independence and is frequently used for ceremonies and wreath laying. The statue of Cuauhtémoc, the Aztec emperor who is regarded with great affection by the Mexican people, stands at the spot where the Reforma and Insurgentes Sur intersect.

Zona Rosa

This area, known as the pink zone, starts more or less at the intersection between Reforma and Insurgentes and extends southward to the area of Avenida Chapultepec and Florencia. This part of town with its chic restaurants, hotels, shops and cafes is considered to be the sophisticated part of town and very 'in' with the smart set. The pedestrian zones at Copenhague and Genova Streets are enjoyable spots at which to linger over a meal or drink as you sit at one of the little outdoor restaurants and watch the world go by.

Continuing west, Reforma leads to the beautiful **Bosque de Chapultepec** (Chapultepec Park) which is really several parks in one. It covers a vast area of woods, fields, lakes, museums, playgrounds, picnic areas, an amusement park, fine botanical gardens and a large zoo. The grounds were used as a recreation park by Aztec rulers who first named it Chapultepec, meaning 'Hill of the grasshopper' as a description of the hill on which Chapultepec Castle sits.

Construction on the **castle,** which dominates the park, started in the late 18th century. From the hill it commands a fine view over the Paseo de la Reforma and the city in all its grandeur. After Independence, it became a Military Academy and here some teenage cadets died defending the school when it was stormed by United States troops during the final battle of the U.S./Mexican war in 1847. The monument to those Boy heroes (Niños Heroes) stands in front of the castle and is an impressive feature of the park. When Maximilian became Emperor of Mexico he made the castle his home. After his execution in 1867 the castle continued to be used for some years as the official residence of presidents of Mexico but now the President's official residence is at Los Pinos in the southern part of Chapultepec Wood. The castle is now a National Museum of History displaying many relics of Maximilian's reign and other works of art. You can visit the elegantly furnished apartments of Maximilian and Carlota and there is an outstanding collection of the coaches and carriages used by the rulers of the country. There are several rooms dedicated to different periods of Mexican history from colonial times to the present. Other rooms house specific collections, including coins, clocks, ceramics, pianos. There are hundreds of paintings and many fine murals executed by Mexico's leading artists.

Chapultepec Park is the site of several museums. The most famous of these is the **Museo de Antropologia** (Museum of Anthropology). It was opened in 1964 and this museum is considered to be the finest of its kind in the world, both for its magnificent presentations and its unique collection of pre-Columbian Mexican art. No visitor should miss a visit to this world-renowned museum which was designed around a large patio shaded by a gigantic 'mushroom' — the world's largest expanse of concrete supported by a single pillar. Chambers around the patio are devoted to all the major ancient civilizations of pre-Columbian Mexico. On display you can see, among countless other items, the famous Aztec Calendar Stone, beautifully constructed models of the old Aztec capital called Tenochtitlán, giant Olmec heads from Tabasco, treasures from the tomb of Palenque and the sacred well of the Maya in Yucatán. There are interesting ethnographical displays of the current lives of present-day Indians in Mexico on the second floor. English-speaking guides are available.

Other museums worth visiting in the park area include the **Museo de Arte Moderno** (Museum of Modern Art) which has a collection of paintings by Mexican artists, the **Museo Rufino Tamayo** (Rufino Tamayo Museum) which contains, in addition to some of the master's own works, a large collection of famous contemporary painter's works and the **Galeria de Historia** (Gallery of History) with three-dimensional displays of light and sound scenes depicting the Mexican struggle for liberty.

The park is more than a recreational area — it is an important feature of Mexico City.

Beyond the park, Reforma passes

through one of the most luxurious residential areas, known as **Las Lomas** (the hills). Houses here are built in Californian or pseudo-Spanish colonial styles, with sumptuous gardens and swimming pools. Many of the residents are affluent Mexican businessmen, film stars and diplomats.

Southern Mexico City

Special attractions in the southern part of the city include **Ciudad Universitaria** (University City) which is the campus of the National University of Mexico, located on both sides of Insurgentes Sur. Although it claims to be the oldest University in the continent, its architecture is strikingly modern and the buildings are notable for their vivid exterior murals. The library building is famed for its exterior by Juan O'Gorman which is entirely covered by mosaics and the Rectory by David Siqueiros is also notable for its exterior murals. Across the way, you can see the **Estadio Olimpico** (Olympic Stadium) with excellent murals by Diego Rivera. This was the site of the opening and closing ceremonies as well as other events at the 1968 Olympic Games and it can be used as a soccer stadium. The **Estadio Azteca** (Aztec Stadium) at Calzada Tlalpan, is a most impressive soccer stadium which can accommodate over 100,000 spectators. It is an important venue for the World Cup of 1970 and 1986 as a site for the final itself.

A third stadium, the **Estadio J. Lopez P.** (also known as Neza '86), is located at Ciudad Netzahualcóyotl about 9 miles (15 km) south of the city. Soccer-futbol, as it is called in Mexico, is the national sport.

The pyramids of **Cuicuilco** off Insurgentes, which are near the Olympic Village are believed to be the oldest man-made structures in the Western Hemisphere. Centuries ago, they were buried by Lava from the Xitli volcano, which form the lava beds of Pedregal. Usually the largest pyramid is circular and could have been constructed from astronomical base.

Copilco is a very early pre-Columbian cemetery located off Insurgentes Avenue just before reaching University City. It too was buried under the lava from Xitli Volcano. It was discovered in 1917 and contains a few skeletons, surrounded by early pottery pieces.

The **Siqueiros Polyforum** is located on Insurgentes Sur. This has been developed as a cultural center with a concert hall and theaters for dance and drama. The main feature is a gigantic set of murals by Alfaro Siqueiros entitled *The March of Humanity*.

Beyond this, you can visit the **Plaza México** which is the largest bullring in the world with a capacity for 50,000 people and bullfights take place on most Sundays at 4.30 in the afternoon.

The **Floating Gardens of Xochimilco**, which are about 15 miles (25 km) southeast of the city center, are well worth a visit. Xochimilco is the Aztec word meaning 'in the seed beds' or 'place of the flower fields'. When the Aztecs inhabited the Valley of Mexico, the old capital was built on an island in the middle of Lake Texcoco. They set up strings of rafts to float on the waters, covered them with soil and planted crops. The rafts rooted themselves in the shallow waters and the area has remained a network of canals and gardens producing flowers and vegetables. Gondola-type boats float along decked with flowers while others are used by taco vendors and *mariachi* players. Sunday is the most colorful day to visit the gardens and cruising the area in one of the boats can be fun.

The **Bazar Sábado** (Saturday market) is a great attraction. It is located on Plaza San Jacinto in the San Ángel district and is a Saturday only center, in an elegant building, where sophisticated craftsmen display a wide variety of arts and crafts from all regions of Mexico. The quality is very high and you can buy some very attractive pieces here. There is a pleasant restaurant in the central patio of the building which is very lively and colorful, with marimba players and delicious fresh Mexican tacos made on the spot.

San Ángel is a picturesque village within the city and is a favorite residential area for writers, actors and prominent characters. Some beautiful old colonial

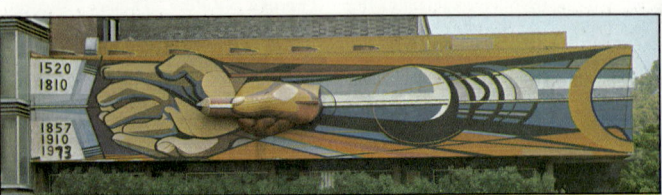

Siqueiros mural at the University

mansions are to be found in the area. The San Ángel Inn was once an old coach stop and is now an outstanding restaurant with a lovely garden and patio. The **Carmen Convent** across from Plaza San Jacinto is a fine monument of colonial times with a unique exhibition of mummies in the crypt. Nearby is the **Casa del Risco** (House of Broken Porcelain), so named for its wonderful fountain of colorful ceramics. This beautiful 18th-century house is also furnished with priceless antiques. The **Museo de Frida Kahlo** (Frida Kahlo Museum) is in nearby Coyoacán district. It was the home and studio of Frida Kahlo who was one of Diego Rivera's wives and a famous painter in Mexico in her own right.

Pedregal is an interesting area to pass by. This was once a lifeless mass of volcanic rock and cacti until an architect devised a method of using the terrain. He constructed a complex of ultra modern houses and made use of the strange lava shapes to model the gardens and swimming pools around them. Today it is one of Mexico's smart residential areas.

Catholics regard the **Basílica de la Virgen de Guadalupe** (Shrine of the Virgin of Guadalupe) as one of the holiest places in the American continent. It is only a few blocks from Insurgentes Norte. Visitors to the Shrine have included Maximilian, President John Kennedy, Charles de Gaulle and Pope John Paul II. The original Basílica, which was gradually sinking into the permeable soil, has been replaced by a modern, circular shaped shrine next door. According to the story, it was here in December 1531 that a simple Indian, named Juan Diego, who had recently been converted to Catholicism, saw a vision of the Virgin Mary. She asked that a church be built in her honor on that spot. Juan Diego relayed this to the local bishop but, understandably, the bishop asked him to bring proof of this. When the Indian returned to the hillside (Tepeyac Hill), on 12 December, the Virgin appeared again and he told her of the bishop's request for proof. She instructed him to gather some roses from a spot which was normally barren and he found the flowers in full bloom, gathered them and hurried to the bishop. When he unfolded his cloak to show the flowers there, the image of the Virgin with dark skin and the features of an Indian was imprinted there. A church was built on the spot and consecrated as a shrine with the Virgin of Guadalupe declared Patroness of Mexico. No one has ever been able to explain the mystery of the image on the Indian's cloak. It is there for everyone to see, unfaded and encased in glass above the central altar of the basilica. This became the first flag of Mexico and was raised as a banner by Father Hidalgo when he marched with his troops at the outbreak of the Independence struggle. Each year, on 12 December there is a National Day of Celebration. Pilgrimages to the shrine are made all year round with many Mexicans from all parts of the country making the last stage of the journey on their knees.

A trip to the Shrine of Guadalupe can be combined with excursions to a number of archaeological sites, churches and convents in the vicinity, including the pyramids at **Teotihuacán,** the **convent of Acolman** and **church of Tepotzotlán.** More details of these destinations can be found under **Central Mexico.** The **Plaza de las Tres Cultures** (Plaza of the Three Cultures) described on p. 41 is also in this area.

Markets and craft centers

Markets are plentiful in Mexico City and you should not miss the opportunity of visiting one or two. They have been used by Mexicans since ancient times when Indians gathered from surrounding areas to meet and sell their wares. Markets are always very busy and very colorful. You are expected to haggle, but this can be fun. Some of the most prominent markets and arts and crafts centers are listed below.

Mercado de La Merced, on Circunvaluación — the biggest market in Mexico. **Centro Artesanal Buenavista,** off Insurgentes Norte behind the Buenavista railway station. This is a huge center selling arts and crafts and jewelry. The **Mercado de la Lagunilla** on Calle Rayón, one block from New Reforma, is open on Sunday mornings only. Everything imaginable is on sale here. The **Bazar Sábado** (Saturday Market), which takes place on Saturdays only, at the Plaza San Jacinto in San Ángel on the south of the city, offers a wide selection of outstandingly high-quality arts and crafts.

Sundays in Mexico City

It is fun to spend a Sunday in Mexico City. The swell of weekday traffic subsides and the city becomes alive with local residents out and about, enjoying their day of leisure. There are many special attractions available to tourists on Sundays. Band concerts are held in Alameda Park and in Chapultepec Park, where many Mexican families take their weekly outing — picnicking, boating on the lake or just strolling around. The Floating Gardens of Xochimilco is also a pleasant destination for a Sunday outing (see p. 46).

Bullfights are staged on most Sundays throughout the year at the Plaza México bullring on the south side of the city (see p.

46). Also on most Sundays, you can watch the *charreadas* at one of the Ranchos in the city. *Charreadas* are Mexican-style rodeos where spectators view excellent displays of horsemanship. The rider's costumes are beautifully embroidered and the show itself is very colorful with *mariachi* bands, singing and regional dancing. Your hotel should be able to tell you where and when the next *charreada* will be held.

Visitors should not miss the opportunity to attend a performance of the spectacular Ballet Folklorico which is staged on Sunday mornings and evenings at the Palacio de Bellas Artes (Palace of Fine Arts). Performances are also held on Wednesday evenings.

Sunday morning is the time to visit the Lagunilla Market on Rayon Street (see p. 47) and there is an interesting display of paintings by contemporary artists at Sullivan Park which is two blocks north of the Reforma on the Insurgentes intersection.

Entertainment

Mexico City offers a wide range of restaurants to suit visitors of every nationality and eating out is usually a pleasurable experience. There are numerous Mexican restaurants serving good, authentic local specialties. The atmosphere is usually informal and lively and a visit can be great fun. American-style chains, which are normally inexpensive, also offer Mexican food and the majority of restaurants include some Mexican specialities on their menu. Many fine international restaurants specialize in dishes from Spain, France, Switzerland and Italy and there are good Oriental restaurants serving Polynesian, Japanese and Chinese dishes.

Most of the fashionable restaurants are located in the Zona Rosa and in some of the top class hotels. These can be very sophisticated and can usually be found in an interesting setting with attractive decor and excellent food. They can also be quite expensive. Most of the fashionable restaurants fill up quickly, especially at night, and you can avoid disappointment by booking in advance. For Mexicans the most important meal of the day is lunch, which often revolves around business meetings, whereas dinner is much more of a social and family affair. Lunch can last from about 2 pm and continue until 6 or 7 in the evening, or even later! Most restaurants stay open all afternoon and when you arrive for dinner in the early evening you may still find people left over from lunch. Mexicans would generally start dinner at about 9 pm or even later. Formal attire is appreciated in good restaurants in Mexico City and gentlemen are expected to wear a suit and tie.

During the day, there is little music in restaurants but there is often some sort of music in the evenings, from soft piano background music or romantic violins to rousing traditional Mexican songs.

Major hotels have at least one cocktail bar, usually with some type of entertainment and each with its own character. Some bars have a full evening's entertainment of regional songs and dances or a show with singers or dancers. Bars stay open quite late and a visit to one of these can be a pleasant way to round off your evening after dinner. Nightclubs can be more expensive. In the evenings, you can take a trip to the **Pyramids of Teotihuacán** where there is a light and sound show every night at 7 pm except Mondays. An evening visit to the **Plaza Garibaldi** is to be recommended for those who would like to listen to the *mariachi* bands which gather there every night en masse. They will play for you on order but each song costs! There are several bars along the square although they can be a bit rough. *Jai-alai* (or *frontón*), regarded by some as the fastest game in the world, is played most evenings at the ***Frontón México.*** If you wish to make excursions from Mexico City, please see chapter four which describes towns and sites in the surrounding area.

Festivals and Events: there are a large number of festivals in Mexico City and the most notable fiestas are listed here. Sept 15-16, Independence Day. At 11 pm on the evening of the 15th, the President of Mexico appears on the balcony of the National Palace and gives the *Grito* (Cry of Liberty) pronounced by Father Hidalgo in 1810. The multitude in the zócalo sings the National Anthem and chants 'Viva Mexico' and there are spectacular fireworks. This signals the start of the celebrations of Independence which continue on the 16th with military parades and locals dress in their regional costumes; Nov 20, Anniversary of the 1910 Revolution. Celebrations and a parade; Dec 12, Feast Day of the Virgin of Guadalupe, the patroness of Mexico. Songs and dances from all over the country are performed in front of the shrine. Mexicans make pilgrimages to the shrine in almost endless processions around this date; Dec, Christmas festivities. This is a most festive month in Mexico City. The city sparkles with decorations and lights and there is a party atmosphere. Every night, between Dec 16 and 24, families and neighbors get together to re-enact in song and verse the search for shelter at the *posada* (inn), carrying images of Joseph and Mary and lighted candles. Then follows a festive party of singing, dancing and drinking.

THE SOUTH

This area, covering Guerrero, Oaxaca and Chiapas, is undoubtedly one of the most fascinating and beautiful regions of Mexico, with dramatic changes in climate, terrain and culture from one state to another. Guerrero and Oaxaca are states characterized by majestic mountain ranges stretching far into the distance and by beautiful valleys, fertile plains and an abundance of all varieties of cacti. The mighty mountain range of the Sierra Madre del Sur, which dominates these states, merges and dissolves into the forest-covered highlands of Chiapas, deep in the south of Mexico. The entire coastline has a natural beauty: it has wide curving bays, rocks and inlets, long stretches of golden sand and pounding breakers set against the striking background of the mountains. A few resorts have sprung up over the years, some much more developed than others, but much of the coast is still completely untouched and retains its virgin beauty. In Chiapas it can be cool and fresh in the highlands and it rains much more here than in any other part of the land. Chiapas has lush green vegetation, hidden rivers, cascades and waterfalls, multihued lagoons of stunning beauty, exotic birds, butterflies and a rich flora and fauna.

Many travelers pass through the state of Guerrero to reach Acapulco — the famous resort on the south coast. As a result, the

area has become more attuned to the 20th century as we know it than most other parts of Mexico.

Visitors should know that the interior of southern Mexico also has much to offer, particularly in the historical sense. In the latter half of the 15th century, Aztec troops were sent to control trade and established a fort in the center of Oaxaca Valley. In 1521, the Spaniards arrived and attempted to take control, but they were unable to subdue the Aztecs, the Zapotecs — who had inhabited the valley since prehistoric times — and the Mixtecs. Today, the Aztec and Zapotec languages are still spoken in many villages. Only when the Spaniards, led by Cortés, had conquered the Aztec capital, Tenochtitlán, could a force of sufficient strength be mustered to subjugate the inhabitants of Oaxaca. During 300 years of colonial rule which followed, the Spaniards built attractive towns, cities and exquisite churches and one of the finest examples of their architecture is the hillside town of Taxco which is preserved as a National Monument.

The area is rich in historical heritage and there is an abundance of archaeological treasure. The ruins of Monte Albán and Mitla, which are among the most important centers, should not be missed and local museums have displays of artifacts found in the region.

Agriculture forms the basis of Oaxaca's economy. Local produce includes coffee, rubber, pineapple, tobacco and sugar. Many local people became artisans and craftsmen over the years and Oaxaca has gained fame as an arts and crafts center, renowned for its 'black' pottery which is only produced here, made from the clay in the area. Oaxaca is also the home of the fiery *mezcal* drink. The 'magic mushroom' with its strange hallucinogenic properties grows wild in the surrounding mountains and has long been used by Indians for med-

Indian Feather Dancer, Oaxaca

icinal and curative purposes, as well as for social and religious rites. Both the states of Oaxaca and Chiapas are essentially Indian in character. The Maya were probably the greatest of the ancient civilizations, inhabiting the southeastern area, extending down into Central America and they left thousands of sites, many of which are well worth visiting since their restoration. The ruins of Palenque, which are perhaps the most magnificent of all, and other lesser sites are set deep in the dense jungles of Chiapas, allowing the visitor to feel something of the thrill of stumbling by chance upon lost cities of a bygone era. The Lacandon Indians, who are descendants of the Maya, and many other groups — some in danger of vanishing altogether — inhabit the remote jungles, speaking in their own languages. Ancient customs are still practiced with little evidence of the influences of modern times. The region is very much more remote and inaccessible than its neighboring states and it is this which gives it a great appeal to the adventurous traveler with a taste for the unknown and the unexpected.

Gastronomic specialities: on the coast there is an abundance of fresh seafood such as lobster, oyster, dark-meat fish, pargo (snapper or sea bass) and ceviche acapulqueno — a cocktail of fish marinated in lime juice. In Oaxaca and Chiapas, the local cuisine is mainly Indian with some other influences. Oaxaca produces a richer, darker *mole* than in other parts, usually served with pork rather than chicken and the tamale is larger, flat and not so dry as elsewhere. (For a description of traditional Mexican dishes, see p. 20.) Chiapas is famed for its wild duck, roast boar, iguana stew, chille, olives, chicken and sopa de pan — pieces of bread soaked in chicken broth and served with raisins. Unfortunately, restaurants tend to offer more international dishes and these local

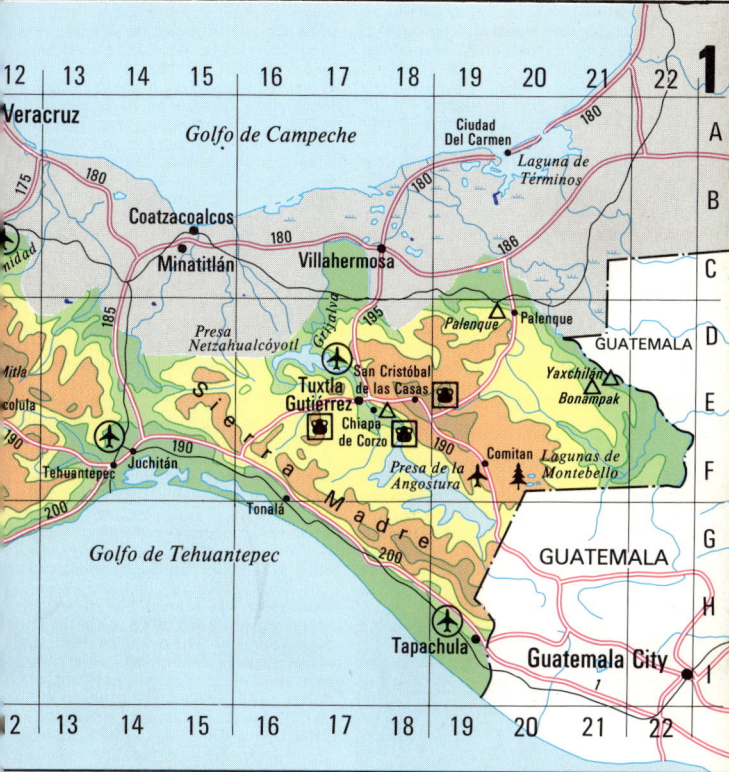

specialities are prepared more often in the home.

Festivals and events: Jan 1, Mitla — Zapotec Indians celebrate New Year's Eve with an all-night vigil (Oaxaca); Jan 20, Chiapa de Corzo, San Sebastian Day — fairs, folk dances (Chiapas); Apr 1–7, fair commemorating the founding of the town of San Cristóbal de las Casas (Chiapas); May 15–25, Juchitán Spring Festival — native dancing (Oaxaca); May 31, Tehuantepec Regional Arts and Crafts Fair (Oaxaca); mid July, Lunes del Cerro (Monday of the Hill) — Aztec and Christian Festival, dancers, including the famous *Danza de las Plumas* (Indian feather dance) on a hill top at Cerro del Fortín (Oaxaca); July 7–15, San Fermin Festival of Lights at Comitán (Chiapas); Dec 16–25, Christmas week — fireworks, regional dances, ceremony of lights; Dec 23, Noche de los Rabanos (Night of the Radishes), Oaxaca (Oaxaca). In this ever-changing country, it is wise to check details of dates and times of events with the Mexican Tourist Office.

Acapulco E5

Guerrero (pop. 700,000). The meaning of the Indian word Acapulco is 'The Place where the Reeds were destroyed'. Mexico's most famous resort lies on the Pacific Coast due south of Mexico City. By road, traveling time from Mexico City is about 4½ hours and the journey lasts only 35 minutes by air. Proximity to Mexico City, coupled with Acapulco's year-round sunshine, were major factors in attracting the first few Mexican visitors who ventured forth in the 1920s in search of a little relaxation by the sea. With the construction of a proper road and the appearance of a few modest boarding houses, interest began to grow. The first hotel was opened in 1934, but tourism only really started to have any significance when an airport was built linking it daily with the capital and when a new superhighway was completed in 1955. From then on, Acapulco has never looked back.

Today it has acquired a reputation as a glittering playground for the jet set and continues to attract visitors from all over the world. Acapulco, which was founded by the Spaniards in 1530, began to gain importance as a trading port with links between Mexico and the Orient. Boats laden with ivory, porcelain, silks and perfumes would arrive regularly from the Philippine Islands, China and Japan. The goods would be transported by mule to Mexico City, down to the Gulf port of Veracruz and shipped off to Spain. This became a very profitable route and before long pirates lurking in the surrounding waters began plundering the precious cargoes. The Fort of San Diego was built to protect Acapulco Port against the invaders. It was destroyed by an earthquake in 1776 but was rebuilt and remains one of the oldest buildings in Acapulco. After the Mexicans gained their Independence from the Spaniards in 1821, trading ceased and Acapulco reverted to a sleepy fishing village until the gradual growth of tourism converted it into the Acapulco of today.

As a bend in the mountain road reveals the bay below, the first view of Acapulco

Acapulco Bay

fairly takes your breath away. Towering mountains surround a graceful wide curving bay of blue sparkling water. Glittering high-rise hotels line the long stretch of golden sands, thick with palm trees. Its natural setting bears a resemblance to the French Riviera. The older and prettier part of Acapulco on the western side of the bay became less fashionable with the advent of increasingly more luxurious hotels along the stretch of bay on the eastern side. Each year or so a new property

seems to appear and to extend the long line of buildings a little further. Visitors tend to prefer relaxing around the hotel pools where most of the 'action' is centered, rather than swimming in the sea which is more often favored by Mexicans. If it seems that Acapulco has everything you could wish for during the day, with its countless possibilities for all forms of water sport such as water-skiing, parasailing, surfing, fishing, sailing etc, it really comes alive at night. Visitors fill the open air bars to watch the sun go down and see Acapulco light up. They enjoy the lively restaurants and dancing the night away in any one of the numerous 'in' discos.

The architecture and setting for gardens and pools gives each hotel a character of its own and a few can be considered outstanding. Las Brisas (the Breezes), a unique complex of small bungalows built up a hillside with private swimming pools, commands a spectacular view of Acapulco Bay by day, or by night when the bay shimmers like a jewel to the reflection of myriads of twinkling lights. Everything at the hotel is pink — including the pink and white striped jeeps — and with its incredibly romantic setting, it has rightly earned itself a name as the Honeymoon Hotel. The fashionable and stylish Villavera Hotel also has private bungalows and swimming pools and is the site of the first bar-in-the-pool. The Acapulco Princess is a stunning creation of modern architecture. Built in the shape of a pyramid, with a flower-filled entrance reaching up to the roof, it has exotic tropical grounds and swimming pools, designed for pure pleasure. Guests are in a world of their own here and some never feel the need to leave the grounds. There are a large number of hotels ranging from deluxe to inexpensive and camping is available.

One of Acapulco's greatest attractions is the unique spectacle of the famous div-

The divers of La Quebrada

Sunset at Acapulco

ers of La Quebrada who leap from a height of about 135 ft (40 m) into the shallow waters of the swirling Pacific below. This is even more dramatic at night when the scene is lit up by flares.

A short trip to see the vivid sunsets at **Pie de la Cuesta** beach, where great rollers crash onto the shores, is well worthwhile. Acapulco provides an excellent opportunity to totally relax in the sunshine and to take advantage of the many enjoyable activities which abound for the pleasure-seeker. *Mexico City 253 mi/407 km.*

Chiapa de Corzo   E18
Chiapas (pop. 28,000). Former capital of Chiapas. The ruins at Chiapa de Corzo, about 9 miles (15 km) from Tuxtla Gutiérrez, are comparatively unknown to tourists but have great archaeological significance. This was one of the earliest known settlements of the Maya and is thought to go back some 3000 years when it was an important trading center, serving as a link between the Maya in the east and the Zapotecs in the west. The picturesque village of Chiapa de Corzo overlooks the River Grijalva and commands a spectacular view of the gorge. The town was founded in 1528 on the site of an Indian settlement. There is a remarkable fountain in the main square, built in the form of the King of Spain's crown. There is a small museum of popular arts and crafts. Local crafts include lacquered gourds, ceramics, hand embroidered fabrics, carved wooden masks and marimbas. The annual Easter Carnival, where the Parachico dancers perform in great numbers with masks and colorful costumes, takes place here. This is the point of departure for an exciting river trip to the Chicoasen Dam through the 26 mile (42 km) long, 6000 ft (1830 m) deep **Sumódero Canyon** carved out by the turbulent waters and rapids of the River Grijalva. Its walls can rise up to 3300 ft (1000 m). Suitable for the adventurous. This is quite wild country, said to be inhabited by the ghosts of the Indians who are supposed to have flung themselves into the raging waters below rather than surrender to the unwelcome Spanish visitors. *Tuxtla Gutiérrez 9 mi/15 km.*

Chilpancingo   D6
Guerrero (pop. 70,000). State capital. This was the site of the very first Mexican Congress in 1813. Primarily an agricultural center and quiet little mountain town with a few buildings of interest; the State Capitol on the main square, the Asunción Church and the old cemetery. *Acapulco 82 mi/132 km.*

Comitán   F19
Chiapas (pop. 45,000). Comitán was once the site of the most populated Mayan Qhiche Kingdom in southeast Chiapas. Now, with only a small community, it is the chief entry port for goods from Guatemala and the main market center for the Tzeltal Indians. The architecture is colonial and there are stunning views of the area from the houses which are built on

huge rocks and linked by very steep winding streets up the hillside. The area abounds with thousands of varieties of orchid.

A drive of about two hours brings you to a beauty spot of Chiapas. In one of the most remote areas of the country, located near the border with Guatemala, there are the **Lagunas de Montebello** (Lakes of Montebello). There are about 60 lakes with crystal-clear waters of all colors and hues from turquoise and light blue to almost blue-black shades. They cover a huge area in the jungle.

The Lacandon Indians inhabit the surrounding forests and the area has an atmosphere all of its own, strangely silent and remote. This was declared a National Park by the Government in 1960 to preserve its wild and natural beauty and there are plans to develop it in time or to make it more accessible to the visitor. *Tuxtla Gutiérrez 106 mi/171 km.*

Iguala B6

Guerrero (pop. 90,000). Important agricultural center with an interesting market on Fridays where local Indians sell their goods. It has a pleasant town church and a pretty zócalo full of trees. The Mexican flag was created here and raised in proclamation of Mexico's Independence from the Spaniards in 1821. *Taxco 22 mi/35 km.*

Ixtapa C2

Guerrero. Recently developed seaside resort on the Pacific Coast, north of Acapulco. The resort is a creation of FONATUR, the agency set up by the Mexican government a few years ago to develop new areas for tourism and to create work for the local population. Not long ago Ixtapa was merely a long strip of sand bordered by jungle. The little fishing village of **Zihuatanejo** lies just a few miles away. Instead of extending this little resort, it was decided to build a brand new resort nearby with a modern infrastructure, new roads, drains, electrical power etc. With its long stretch of sandy beaches, hotels of all categories and a golf course, it has gradually grown in popularity over the years, with a special appeal for family holidays. Visitors who would like some 'local color' can make the short trip over to Zihuatanejo. A new highway is planned which will link the area to Mexico City and the trip should take about five hours. An international Airport serves both resorts. Sometimes listed together as one resort — Ixtapa/Zihuatanejo — they are, in fact, two quite separate places and should be regarded as such. *Acapulco 157 mi/253 km.*

Oaxaca D11

Oaxaca (pop. 115,000). State capital known as the 'jade city'. Architecture is colonial but the inhabitants are predominantly Indian. Set on a plateau in the Valley of Oaxaca, this charming city has a specially attractive character. There is a certain luminosity in the air and the colors of the distant mountains, which are shrouded in mist in the early mornings, are constantly changing to form a unique background. 'The place covered with trees' is a Zapotec Indian name for the town now known as 'Oaxaca'. The Spaniards established Oaxaca, which they conquered in the 1520s, as capital of the state and Cortés, their leader, was rewarded by Charles V of Spain with substantial land and the title 'Marquis del Valle de Oaxaca' — a grant which remained within his family until the Revolution in 1910.

Oaxaca's main square, or zócalo, is one of the most colorful in Mexico. There is a bandstand where musical concerts are given in the evenings and on Sunday afternoons and there is plenty of marimba which is the typical music of this region. Benches and graceful trees surround the square and you can visit sidewalk cafés under the arcades. The zócalo is a meeting place for everyone, from the Oaxaqueños and the local Indian population with their colorful 'sarapes' or shawls to tourists, students and street vendors.

At the end of the zócalo is the cathedral on which building began in the 16th century. It was completed in the 18th century. The cathedral was a gift to the city of Oaxaca from the King of Spain. The 17th-century Church of La Soledad has a richly carved façade and a famous statue of the Patron Saint of Oaxaca, the Virgen de la Soledad, who is said to have worked many miracles. Santo Domingo is an impressive church, founded by the Dominican Fathers in 1570, and it has one of the most magnificent Baroque interiors in Mexico. Gold chandeliers hang from the ceilings and the floors are paved with tiles. The walls are richly inlaid with gold scroll and polychrome reliefs set against a white background. Its eleven chapels form an outstanding example of Baroque art.

The Rufino Tamayo Museum of pre-Hispanic art is about four blocks from the zócalo. This colonial building once housed the state archives and is now the home of a wonderful collection of archaeological pieces donated by Rufino Tamayo, a native of Oaxaca and one of Mexico's most famous artists. The regional museum of Oaxaca also has a fine collection of treasures from the area such as priceless jewels found at Monte Albán and examples of regional arts and crafts.

Oaxaca is famous throughout Mexico for its **Saturday market.** It takes place outside the city center in the southwestern outskirts and is well worth a visit. Hundreds of Indians gather here from all the surrounding towns and villages and sell their wares, from exotic fruits, vegetables and meats, to pottery, ceramics, local garments and herbs and potions to cure maladies. There is much hustle and bustle, color and noise.

Many other Indian villages in the vicinity are worth visiting for their colorful weekly markets and among the most attractive are **Ocotlán,** Fridays and **Tlacolula,** Sundays.

Mitla, 'Place of Rest', lies 24 miles (39 km) southeast of Oaxaca, just off the Pan American highway. This fine example of the Mixtec civilization was once an important religious center with catacombs beneath the buildings. Some of Mexico's rarest remains are to be found here: palace walls covered with ornamentation and thousands of mosaics made of tiny stones to form geometrical patterns of coils alternating with key designs symbolizing the stylized image of the Plumed Serpent. The Mixtecs swept down to this area from what is now known as Central Mexico and reached the peak of their culture in the 13th century. Unlike most other archaeological sites in the land which fell into decay over the centuries and needed restoration, Mitla has remained much as it was some thousand years ago and very little restoration work has been necessary. The Mixtecs were fine artisans and produced beautiful jewelry in particular. The Frisell Museum in the village of Mitla is worth visiting to see a collection of artifacts from the area.

Near the tiny village of Santa Maria de Tule, stands the celebrated 135 ft (41 m) high **Tule Tree** which has the largest circumference in the world — about 164 ft (50 m). It is a most impressive sight, appearing to be a bundle of trunks springing from the same roots, and it may be the oldest living thing in Mexico.

Ancient walls of Mitla

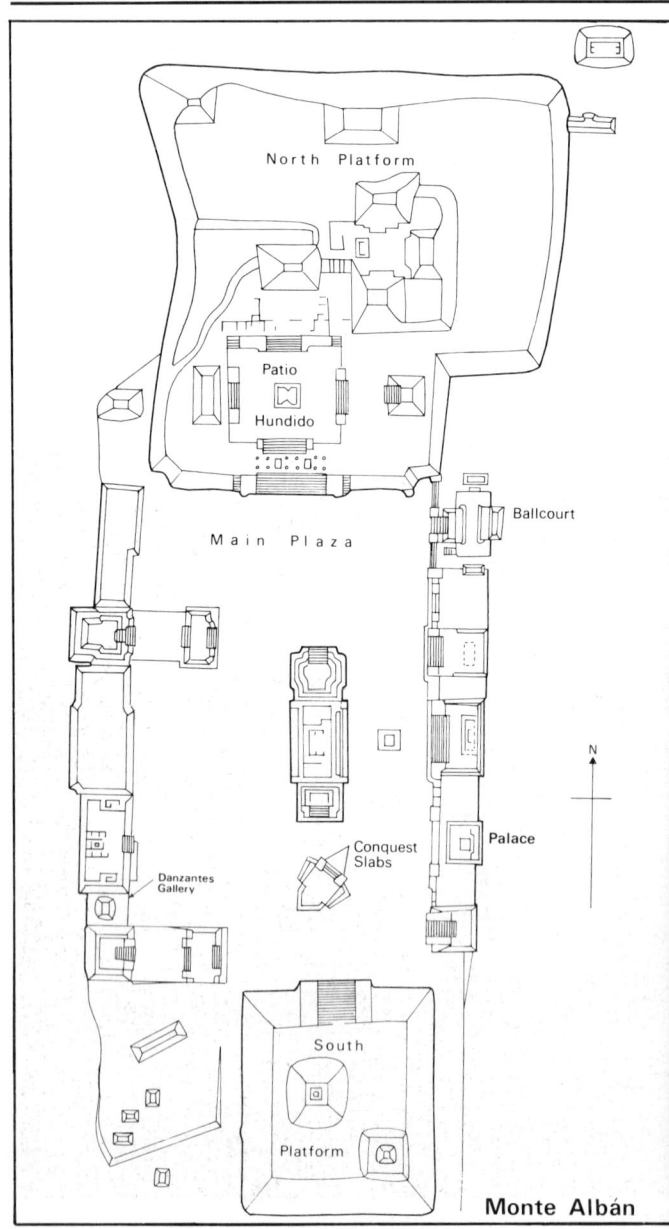

Other notable ruins in the vicinity are **Yagul** which is on a hilltop, **Lambityeco,** and the partially excavated ruins of **Dainzu,** all in the vicinity of Oaxaca town. **Monte Albán** — the White Hill — is situated about 6 miles (10 km) southwest of Oaxaca on a mountain plateau, and overlooks the city. Covering an area some 1000 by 800 ft (300 by 240 m) on a flat hilltop ringed by mountains, the setting for this white acropolis is spectacular.

Monte Albán dates back several hundred years before the Christian era and was developed by the Zapotecs as a 'City of the Gods'. They occupied it until around AD300 and the city probably had as many as 50,000 inhabitants at the height of its importance. The Mixtecs later invaded the area, took over Monte Albán and, around the year 1000, they began using it as a regal cemetery. The center consists of a great central 'square', various buildings, temples, a ballcourt and tombs. During the continuing excavations, archaeologists have uncovered numerous paintings, cases and, in one tomb, dazzling treasures of gold jewelry, quartz, turquoise and pottery which it is said are comparable to the findings at the tomb of Tutankhamen. One of the most interesting and baffling features of Monte Albán are strange carvings depicting the *Danzantes*, or Dancers, on stone slabs. Experts are puzzled by their significance. They show deformed persons which may suggest that they are medical specimens. The heads, in profile, also depict features of a range of races, from the roman noses of the Indian to characters with negroid features, indicating ancient links with the African continent. On the southeast of the square, the ball court which was used in those times for the popular ball game, resembles a modern stadium. *Mexico City 315 mi/507 km.*

Mask of Xipe Totel, Monte Albán

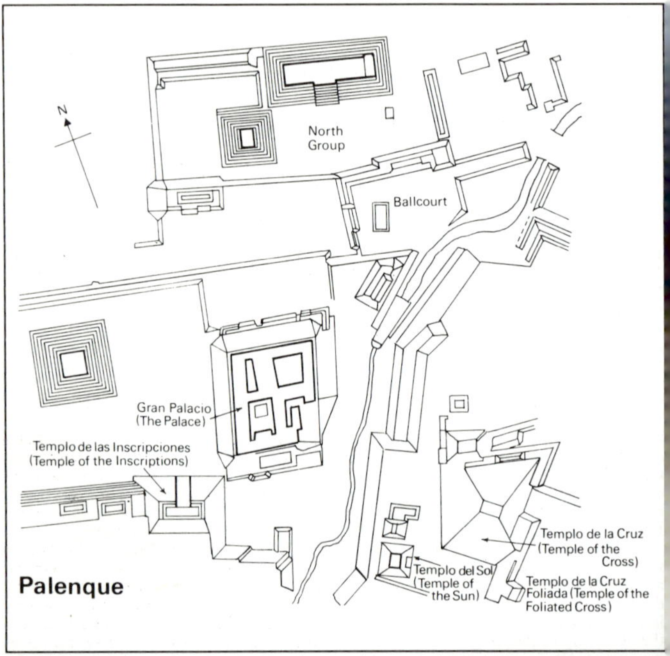

The South

One of the most spectacular of all Mayan sites in Mexico: the ruins of the Palace of Palenque are surrounded by wild, green jungle

Palenque   D19

Chiapas. The name is derived from the word meaning 'palisade'. This is perhaps the most sensational of the Mayan sites. The ancient city, set deep in the mountain jungles of the south and surrounded by dense green vegetation, has a brooding air of mystery. It is situated just above the plain of the River Usumacinta at the foot of a chain of hills and is considered one of the great cities of the classical Mayan period which flourished from the 7th to the 10th century. One of its most important pyramids is el Templo de las Inscripciones (Temple of the Inscriptions) which dominates the site and has been the object of important excavations. In 1952, a French archaeologist discovered a crypt in the temple containing the remains of a great chieftain surrounded by jewels and rich jade ornaments. This tomb is the only discovery of its kind to have been found in a pyramid within Mexico. Other important buildings are el Templo del Sol (the Temple of the Sun), el Templo de la Cruz (the Temple of the Cross), el Templo de la Cruz Foliada (the Temple of the Foliated Cross) and el Gran Palacio (the Palace).

The largest of the buildings is the Palace which stands upon a large terrace and has a complex of courts and inner chambers, dominated by a square tower. There is an impressive view from the tops of some of the pyramids, of the green jungles stretching far into the distance. A good museum on the site houses many of the artifacts and treasures of the region.

You can visit **Bonampak,** the City of the Painted Walls, by taking a chartered light aircraft from Palenque, Tuxtla Gutiérrez or Villahermosa. Situated deep in the remote jungles of eastern Chiapas, near the Lacanha River, this was the site of an ancient ceremonial center. It was still being used as a place of worship by the Lancandon Indians, descendants of the Maya, at the time of its discovery in 1946 by an American who spent many years living among the natives.

Bonampak is famous for its detailed painted murals depicting battle scenes, victory celebrations of the first Mayan Empire and musicians and dancers wearing strange masks of lizards and other creatures. The profiles of the characters bear a strong resemblance to pictures found in ancient Egypt.

Yaxchilán is also a site of some importance in the remote jungles of this area. At least at present, the ruins are accessible only by small plane or by special river trips. The site is noted for its intricate stucco baroque roof decorations. *Villahermosa 89 mi/143 km.*

Puerto Angel   G11

Oaxaca (pop. 6000). Puerto Angel is a small seaside resort on the south coast of the state of Oaxaca. Modest accommodations, rustic, undeveloped. Can be reached by road from Puerto Escondido. *Oaxaca 147 mi/237 km.*

Puerto Escondido   G10

Oaxaca (pop. 12,000). This little resort, south of Oaxaca, is still comparatively unspoiled. It is appealing for those seeking a quiet spot with sandy beaches, good fishing and simple accommodations. Visitors should take advantage of its present natural attractions and make the trip before developments get underway, which could be in the forseeable future. It can be reached from Oaxaca by road or small plane or from Acapulco by road. *Oaxaca 163 mi/263 km.*

San Cristóbal de las Casas   E18

Chiapas (pop. 50,000). A two hour drive east of Tuxtla Gutiérrez brings you to the fascinating little town of San Cristóbal de las Casas, home of the Chamula Indians. Situated high in the mountains, there can be breezes during the day and it can be cold at night. The town itself has a Spanish layout but it is inhabited by Indians. Many different Indian groups from the surrounding hills come into town and fill the main square and marketplace, each dressed in the costumes of their own tribe and speaking a different language. Of the many groups in this region the Chamulas, easily recognizable with their handwoven hats of straw held under the chin, are predominant. The Zinacantan Indians are striking with their very short white or pale pink tunics, which enable them to show off their muscular legs. The arrival of the Blom couple who came to live among the Indians and study their way of life, customs and languages is an important event in the area's history.

Mrs. Blom, now a widow, continues to live here and runs the Na Balom Institute, dedicated to the natives of Chiapas, which serves as a museum and a guest house and has many other functions. You should be cautious about taking photographs of the natives, who tend not to like it, and you are advised to ask their permission first, in sign language if necessary. *Tuxtla Gutiérrez 52 mi/83 km.*

Tapachula   I19

Chiapas (pop. 145,000). Only 11 miles (18 km) from the border with Guatemala, this town is a center for coffee, cotton, cocoa and banana plantations. It is located at the foot of the extinct Taconaha volcano, and has a charming little zócalo. *Oaxaca 415 mi/668 km.*

Taxco **B5**

Guerrero (pop. 45,000). Taxco is a beautiful example of Spanish architecture from colonial times with its narrow, cobblestone streets winding their way up the hillside and whitewashed houses with red tiled roofs. It has been declared a National Monument to preserve the style of this period. In the 18th century, a gentleman of French-Spanish origin, Don José de la Borda, came to Taxco and made his fortune from the silver in the area. As a token of his appreciation, he created one of the most attractive churches in the land, bequeathing it to God with the saying 'God gives to Borda, now Borda gives to God'. The Santa Prisca Church, standing on the side of the main square, is built from the pink stone of the region, and is richly inlaid with gold ornaments. It is an outstanding feature of Taxco. De la Borda also built a beautiful town house near the church, the Palacio Borda.

Silverware store, Taxco

The silver mining industry gradually went into decline until the advent of more modern equipment in recent times. In 1929 an American professor arrived on the scene to write a book, became interested in developing the industry and formed classes to craft the silver under the expertize of goldsmiths from neighboring Iguala. The silver industry flourished rapidly and earned Taxco the reputation as silver capital of the world. The town is a shopper's paradise with hundreds of little shops crammed full of beautifully crafted silverware and jewelry. Enchanting by day, Taxco becomes a glittering jewel at night as the hillside is lit up by a myriad of twinkling lights.

Taxco

A short trip can be made from Taxco to visit the stunning caverns of **Cacahuamilpa**. They are the largest of their kind in Mexico and are very impressive. The caverns containing stalactites, stalagmites, arches and boulders are cleverly illuminated. *Mexico City 102 mi/164 km.*

Tehuantepec   F13

Oaxaca (pop. 23,000). The name of the town means 'Jaguar Hill'. One of the two major cities where the land mass narrows to form the Isthmus. Here the Gulf of Mexico and the Pacific Ocean are only 140 miles (225 km) apart. From time to time there have been plans to build a canal and link the seas, but nothing has materialized so far. There is a good railway system between the two oceans which is used for industrial purposes. The women of Tehuantepec, which comes close to having a matriarchal society, are known for their grace and beauty, enhanced by the elaborate and colorful costumes of the region. *Oaxaca 156 mi/251 km.*

Tuxtla Gutiérrez   E17

Chiapas (pop. 200,000). Capital of Chiapas, Tuxtla Gutiérrez is the home of the famous marimba music and as well as being the site for tobacco plantations, it is a prosperous distribution center for the coffee industry. The Palacio de Gobierno (Government Palace) is a fine building of Mexican and Spanish design. It has a museum with well-displayed pre-Hispanic treasures and there is a small but interesting zoo containing animals from the region such as monkeys, jaguars, anteaters, ocelots, boars and various types of birds. Local craftsmen produce inlaid wooden boxes, lacquered gourds, leather goods, jewelry and fine filigree work. The city is rather modern in character. *Oaxaca 337 mi/542 km.*

Chiapas

Zihuatanejo   C2

Guerrero (pop. 10,000). A little fishing village of great charm, about 4½ hours up the coast from Acapulco. Although some changes have gradually come about in recent years, remains comparatively untouched with virtually no modern or high rise buildings. The hotels are hidden, for the most part, in the luxuriant foliage tumbling down to the beaches. The downtown area has several fun restaurants and boats can take you to an excellent beach across the bay, **Playa las Gatas** (the Cats). This has a natural off-shore coral reef and the snorkeling in these crystal-clear, calm waters is superb. A particularly attractive feature of life here is the very informal and relaxing atmosphere. *Mexico City 395 mi/636 km.*

Hut of the Indios, Chiapas

THE YUCATÁN PENINSULA

The three states, Yucatán, Quintana Roo and Campeche together form the Yucatán Peninsula, a mass of land which completes the 'horn-shape' of Mexico, rising in an upward curve into the Gulf of Mexico and the Caribbean Sea. Sandy beaches, many archaeological sites and vast expanses of jungle figure prominently in this large area. There are also lakes and swamps and numerous underground rivers, wells and caverns. Inland, the weather is normally hot and it can be humid, but the coastal regions are refreshed by cooling breezes from the sea and they have a very pleasant, temperate climate throughout the year. The rainy season occurs during the summer months, but there can be sudden changes of weather on the Caribbean coast at any time of the year. When it does rain, the storms rarely last long.

Yucatán is a flat, limestone plain with scrub-forest vegetation, henequen plantations, thatched adobe huts and magnificent Mayan ruins. Its southern neighbor, Quintana Roo, became a state as recently as 1975 and much of its sparsely populated vast wilderness of thick jungle, swamps and lakes is virtually inaccessible. Ancient Mayan centers are scattered throughout the area but with a few notable exceptions, most of these lie buried in the jungle. The popular Caribbean resorts, Cancún, Cozumel and Isla Mujeres are located in this state and have opened the door to tourism in the area, but the rest of the coastline is mostly deserted and underdeveloped. Campeche, which borders these states to the west, is also underpopulated and has similar terrain to that found in Quintana Roo. While Campeche has an appeal for the hunter of jaguar, ocelot and other wildlife which abounds in the forests, the average traveler passes through this state fairly rapidly on his way further east. It is certainly worth lingering a while, however, as Campeche does have its attractions. Some of the scenery is magnificent, with delightful little fishing villages and quiet sandy beaches and the town of Campeche itself is picturesque.

The Maya first came to the peninsula, possibly as early as 1500 BC. There are many theories as to their origins but these remain open. They built pyramids and temples and gradually reached the peak of their civilization, flourishing in their Classic Period which ended in the 10th century. The Mayan empire included Yucatán, Quintana Roo, Campeche, Chiapas and part of Tabasco in Mexico and extended to Guatemala, Belize, Honduras and El Salvador. They excelled at art and architecture and created advanced social and religious concepts. They constructed an observatory to study the stars and reached astonishing levels in their astronomical calculations. Their calendar was more accurate than ours today and they were able to grasp the difficult mathematical concept of zero.

Then, around the year 1000, the warlike Toltecs arrived from the central highlands of Mexico and conquered the Maya. They took over and built onto some of the existing cities, imposing their symbolic carvings over those originally produced by the Maya. Chichén Itzá, which they converted into their capital, is a good example of this. They introduced the practice of offering human sacrifices to their gods and many figures of the *chac-mool*, which were used for these ceremonies, are to be found in Chichén Itzá. A *chac-mool* is a Toltec reclining statue with bent knees, holding a bowl on its stomach which was a receptacle for the torn-out hearts of living victims. From about 1250 there was a gradual decline and the empire began to crumble. By the time the Spaniards arrived in the middle of the 16th century, the once great cities had been abandoned by the Maya and reclaimed by the jungle. Scholars are still trying to unravel the mystery of the Mayan disappearance, whether due to famine, war, natural disaster or other elements, but all theories are mere speculation. The Spaniards arrived in the area in 1528, conquered the existing Maya some years later and built the cities of Campeche and Mérida. The cultivation of henequen, or 'sisal', brought prosperity to landowners who built beautiful palaces and mansions in Mérida which, as a result

The Yucatán Peninsula

of travels to Europe — and France in particular — show influences of French architecture.

After the Spaniards left in 1821, the independent Yucatecans separated several times from Mexico but were finally united for good in 1848. With its rivers, lakes, dense jungles and huge swamps, this whole peninsula was virtually isolated, not only from the rest of Mexico, but also from the neighboring countries to the south. Access to other lands was by sea. Only in recent years, with the completion of airports and a paved highway from Mexico City, was Yucatán able to open its doors to the world and reveal its delights to all who cared to see. Its past isolation has enabled the Yucatán to retain its own identity with its very distinctive characteristics and this is the secret of its charm. For the traveler to Yucatán, the magnificence of its ancient cities rising out of the jungles, the beauty of its Caribbean beaches and the friendliness of its people have made it a favored spot. The most visited Mayan centers are Chichén, Itzá and Uxmal, but there are other important sites in the vicinity: Dzibilchaltún, Kabáh, Sayil and Labná. Visitors can agreeably round off a few days of culture with some relaxation on the Caribbean. There is the choice of the modern, more sophisticated resort of Cancún, or the chance to enjoy the simple pleasures of the little islands of Cozume and Isla Mujeres which lie off the coast of Quintana Roo. As soon as you set foot in the Yucatán Peninsula you cannot fail to sense the warm Yucatecan welcome Yucatecans are direct descendants of the Maya or the Spanish and, in many cases, a mixture of both. They are gentle, courteous and among the most pleasant people in Mexico. They are generally short in stature, and their facial features with almond shaped dark eyes and broad cheeks, leave you in no doubt as to their ancestry.

Many Yucatecans still talk among themselves in the soft tones of the Mayan language, although the majority can speak Spanish as well. With a strong respect for custom and tradition they continue to wear their regional costumes. The men sport the *guayabera*, a neat pin-tucked shirt worn loose and usually white with an embroidered design. The women are dressed in the *huipil*, a loose white shift prettily embroidered and worn over a lace-trimmed underskirt. The little children also dress in this way and, with their round dark eyes, they are quite enchanting. Yucatecans live in small communities in clusters of thatched adobe huts, neatly kept and spotlessly clean.

Principal industries stem from the fiber of henequen, which makes everything from rope and twine to shoes, hammocks, baskets and Chicle chewing gum, and from coconut ranching in Quintana Roo and shrimping in Campeche.

Gastronomic specialities: Yucatán is the home of *chile habanero*, the hottest chilli in Mexico, but the cuisine is normally rather delicate and refined in flavor. *Pibil* dishes are typical of the region, consisting of chicken or pork wrapped in banana leaves, flavored with spices such as bitter oranges, and cooked in an underground oven. *Cochinita pibil* with pork and *pollo pibil* with chicken are special flavors. A non-alcoholic drink of milled rice with vanilla flavoring, named *horchata* is worth tasting. Yucatecan beer is excellent and the more adventurous might like to try *X-Tabentum* which is a Mayan drink of fermented honey flavored with anise. Spanish and French influences can be found in Campeche cuisine; delicacies are *camerones en ajaco*, a spicy shrimp stew, *cangrejo moro*, stone crab, and *esmedregal*, black snapper.

Festivals & Events: Starting Feb or March (Friday preceding Ash Wednesday and continuing until Shrove Tuesday), Mardi Gras with parades, dances, bullfights and cockfights; Dec 12–24, Mérida, Fiesta in honor of Our Lady of Guadalupe (Yucatán). In this ever-changing country, it is wise to check details of dates and times of events with the Mexican Tourist Office.

Campeche   E4

Campeche (pop. 150,000). State capital. An old, fortified town with some ramparts remaining as relics of its colorful past. Pretty little houses of all colors, wrought iron balconies and narrow streets help to form a picturesque city. The whole area is little frequented by tourists which adds to its appeal and it is certainly worth spending some time here. Spaniard Hernández de Córdoba first landed at Campeche in 1517. In following years, a rare logwood dye was discovered in trees in the surrounding forests. A thriving industry, based on this discovery, was formed and Campeche began to prosper. The town's wealth attracted pirates and Campeche became prey to attacks. There was then a period of looting, burning and destruction until, in 1686, work began on a wall and fortresses as protection. This took about 18 years to complete. Two of the main gates and seven of the original fortresses can still be seen today.

The Franciscan Cathedral is the oldest conventional church in the region. It was completed in 1705 after 155 years of construction. The Baluarte Soledad is now an archaeological museum and the Baluarte San Carlos is now an interesting arts and crafts center. In contrast to these impressive old structures Campeche also has some very modern buildings with striking architecture which has inspired their nicknames, such as the Palacio de Gobierno (Government Palace), referred to as the 'jukebox' and the Camara de Diputados (Chamber of Deputies), known as the 'flying saucer'.

Edzná, about 40 miles (65 km) southeast of Campeche, is a major archaeological Mayan site. It dates back to the 7th century and one of its main features is a prominent five story pyramid known as la Gran Acropolis (the Great Acropolis). *Mérida 115 mi/184 km.*

Cancún   B10

Quintana Roo (pop. 55,000). In the language of the Maya, Cancún means 'pot of gold' and in recent times, the development of Cancún has become just as valuable for this previously remote area. It is one of the newest names on the worldwide tourist map and is growing increasingly popular. The island resort of Cancún is situated on the northeast tip of the peninsula. This narrow island, which is about 13 miles (21 km) long, has the Caribbean on one side and a lagoon on the other and it is connected to the mainland by a narrow strip of land. Only a few years ago it was just a long island of soft white sand with palm trees and a hinterland of thick jungle surrounded by water. Then the Mexican government undertook a multi-million dollar development program and set up a trust fund known as FONATUR which funds the programme. After much research this spot was chosen for their first project. As well as creating new resorts to cater for the ever-increasing demands of incoming tourism, the scheme also provided much-needed employment for the local population.

The Yucatán Peninsula

Its convenient location (with access to Florida, which serves as a gateway for flights to numerous destinations), idyllic white beaches and the turquoise waters of the Caribbean were all major factors in selecting Cancún as a site for tourism. Only the two Caribbean islands of Cozumel and Isla Mujeres had previously served this whole peninsula as resorts, somewhat modestly. Over a period of several years a whole new infrastructure was built and Cancún now has proper roads, an international and domestic airport with many daily flights, a wide range of hotels including a number of extremely luxurious properties, a growing downtown area, a modern convention center and it has hosted many meetings and events for people from all over the world, all of which has served to secure Cancún firmly as an international resort. The main attractions are swimming (the cool powder-white sands and the sparkling aquamarine seas of the Caribbean are unbeatable) and water sports such as windsurfing, water skiing, snorkeling, parasailing, sailing and fishing. The waters on the north beach of the island are calmer but it is advisable to adhere to danger warnings and refrain from swimming when you see the red flags which appear particularly on parts of the eastern shore. There is also a fine 18-hole golf course and tennis courts. Most of the good restaurants are in the hotels but there are a number of lively, 'touristy' restaurants downtown and some dancing spots. During the day, most people dress casually in keeping with the semi-tropical weather. Chic dresses are worn at night in top hotels and restaurants but lightweight jackets or ladies shawls are suggested for evenings during the winter months.

You can take a trip to the beautiful **Nichupte Lagoon** where a glass-bottomed boat passes through a jungle canal into the open sea, affording you a glimpse of the

Cancún

varied wildlife here in the exotic marine-world. The government took great pains to preserve the natural beauty of the area and not to upset the ecological balance. Another worthwhile boat trip is to the island of **Contoy,** a wild bird preserve.

Within range of Cancún, there is an abundance of delightful and unexpected places to visit. On the road to Tulum, which lies about two hours south of Cancún by car, there are opportunities for the visitor to stop off at several lovely spots. These can be found by following 'hidden' side roads to the left of this straight ribbon of road and you must watch out for the last minute sign. The first side road worth taking is signed to **Xcaret,** by a tiny wayside restaurant of the same name. A bumpy track into the jungle finally leads you past some small Mayan shrines to a pleasant little rocky cove where you can enjoy a quiet swim and, nearby, a concealed path right in the depths of the jungle leads to one of those marvelous creations of nature which abound in the region — a Mayan *cenote*, or well, formed from a crack in the base of a limestone cliff which projects over it. This path leads to others and you can take a swim in its cool, dark waters where all is silent and a sense of the past prevails.

Further down the road another side road leads to the hotel complex, Club Akumal Carike which consists of little bungalows set among palm trees in the idyllic setting of a perfect Caribbean bay.

The sign **Xel-Ha** leads to another unexpected treat. Here, there are four interlocking lagoons in the forests, each a different shade ranging from emerald greens to azure blues. These crystal-clear waters are partly salty and house countless varieties of exotic tropical fish. Superb for skin diving.

The final reward is **Tulum,** the Mayan walled city. With its magnificent setting of pyramids and temples perched on a clifftop over the sparkling waters of the Caribbean, it is quite different in character from other great Mayan cities. When Tulum was first spotted by the Spaniards as they sailed by the coast in 1518, they were astonished by the sheer size of the city and likened it to Sevilla. It survived long after other Mayan cities had crumbled and were lost to the jungles. The site is dominated by the building known as El Castillo (the Castle). Rare frescoes can be found in the Temple of the Frescoes. One of Tulum's most interesting features is the sculpture carved in a niche in el Templo del Dios Descendente (the Temple of the Descending God). Resembling a diving god, it has given rise to theories of visiting spacemen from other spheres. Down

Tulum

below the ruins, there are superb beaches and good fishing.

The recently discovered ruins of **Coba** are about 30 miles (48 km) inland. It is possible that the whole complex may cover an area greater than that of Chichén Itzá. An increasing number of little hotels which will appeal to fishing enthusiasts are springing up along this coastline.

Communications from Cancún: domestic flights to Mexican cities and international flights to United States cities including direct flights to Miami, Dallas/Fort Worth, Houston, New York and Philadelphia; small planes to Cozumel, Chichén Itzá and Tulum; ferry boats and hydrofoil to Cozumel Island and Isla Mujeres. Accommodations: full range including deluxe. *Mérida 200 mi/321 km.*

Chetumal G8

Quintana Roo (pop. 50,000). State capital. An exotic little jungle town situated on the border with Belize. It is a mecca for Mexicans who come to shop in this free port zone where the shops are crammed with goods from all over the world. There are good opportunities for hunting and the area is unspoiled by tourism. The ruins at **Kohúnlich,** about 45 miles (75 km) away, once formed a Mayan ceremonial center with several structures including el Templo de los Dioses Solares (Temple of the Solar Gods), which is flanked by eight magnificent stucco masks. There is also an extensive plaza, named la Plaza de las Estelas, which has four monolithic stellae. There is some evidence to suggest that this site was inhabited from about 300 BC until the 13th century. There are some beautiful lakes in the vicinity, the largest of which is the long and narrow **Lake Bacalar** with its multihued blue waters. *Mexico City 887 mi/1427 km.*

68 The Yucatán Peninsula

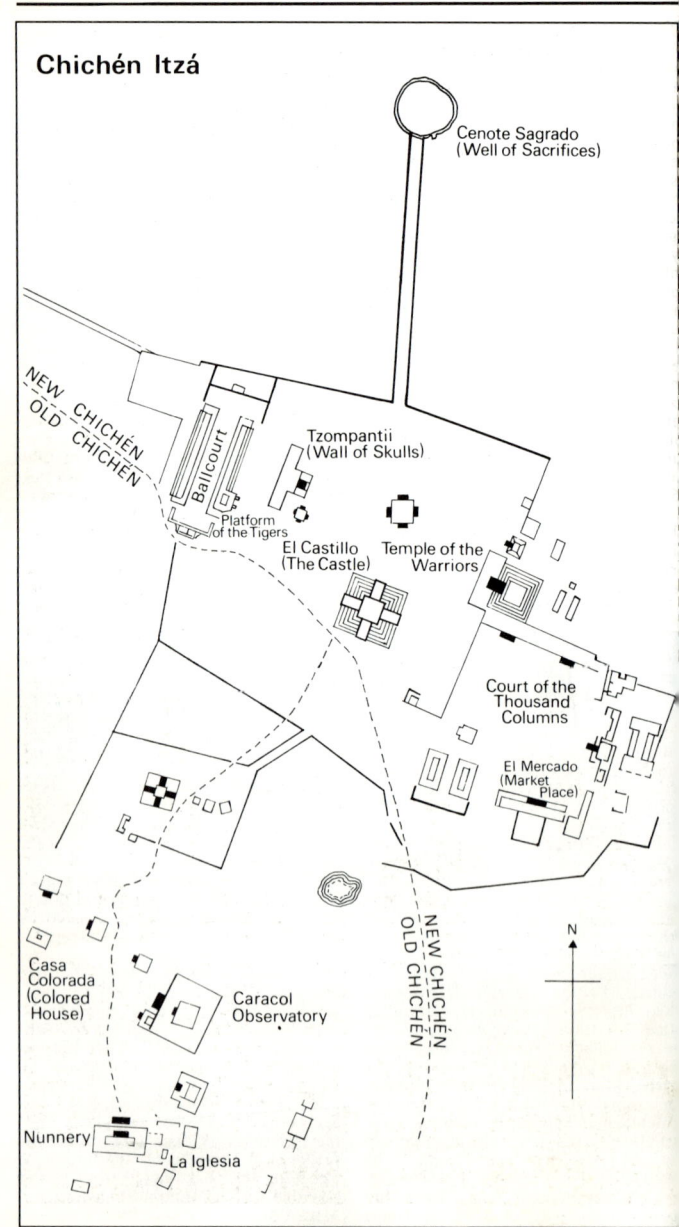

Chichén Itzá C7

Yucatán. The word Chichén is Mayan for 'place of the well' and Itzá refers to a Mayan sect. This magnificent Mayan and Toltec center covers a large area and is considered to be the most famous and complete of Yucatecan ancient cities. It lies about 1½ hour's drive from Mérida and has numerous temples and pyramids, columns and *chac-mools*, spread over large clearings in the jungle form an impressive sight. Initially Chichén Itzá was inhabited by the Itzá tribe, but it gained importance only after the Toltecs settled in the area approximately 1000 years ago and made it their capital. They built onto existing buildings and superimposed their carvings of eagles, warriors and plumed serpents dedicated to their god Quetzalcoatl, known as the Plumed Serpent. Chichén Itzá then flourished as a great center between the 11th and 12th centuries but following a gradual decline in the Mayan culture, the site was abandoned and reclaimed by the jungle by the middle of the 15th century.

The present site is divided into 'New Chichén' and 'Old Chichén'. New Chichén is dominated by the majestic structure known as 'El Castillo' (the castle) with a recumbent *chac-mool* before it. It is built in the shape of a pyramid with a flat, square tower at the top and has four stairways leading up the sides of the building. Each has 91 steps. Together with the top step of the summit, they total 365 — the number of days in the year. A chain handrail enables you to climb up the main stairway to the top from where you have a magnificent view of the site and the green sea of jungle stretching far into the distance. El Castillo was built over a small inner pyramid and you can make your way into its interior for a glimpse of the Red Jaguar encrusted with jade discs. Another *chac-mool* reclines in an adjoining chamber. It's not recommended for those who might suffer from claustrophobia. Some years ago an extraordinary discovery was made by an archaeologist who realised that during the spring and fall equinoxes, the shadows created in the setting sun by the stairway steps on the northwest side of the building, form the body of a serpent, rising, as it were, from the carved heads of Quetzalcoatl at the base of the pyramid. Experts come from all over the world to witness this phenomenon which must have involved amazing mathematics.

Behind El Castillo is the impressive Temple of the Warriors, with its *chac-mools*, carvings of chac masks and its colonnade of warrior-like columns. This extends to the Court of the Thousand

The colorful Rite of Kukulcan is performed on the Sacred Platform at Chichén Itzá. The ruins were inhabited by the Maya and the Toltecs

El Castillo, Chichén Itzá

Chichén Itzá

Columns, representing giant plumed serpents and to El Mercado (the market).

Other buildings of significance are the Tzompantli (Wall of Skulls), Platform of the Eagles and Tigers, and the Temple of the Jaguars, with its ornate decorations depicting jaguars. The Ball Court, which flanks the west side of this temple, is one of the best-preserved and largest in Mexico. The object of the ball game was to propel a solid ball through a high ring of stone without using hands. Carvings on the side of the court suggest the unfortunate members of the losing team were decapitated.

A short walk down a pathway into the jungle leads to the sinister, brooding **Cenote Sagrado** (Well of Sacrifices). The Maya believed that the rain god, Chac, lived here and in periods of drought, sacrificial victims were thrown into the well's murky waters as a gesture of appeasement. Many dredging and diving operations have revealed human bones, countless gold and jade treasures, and hundreds of artifacts.

'Old Chichén' is on the other side of the main road. It is perhaps not as impressive as the 'New Chichén' site but it has some buildings worthy of interest. The Observatory is of great significance. It is also known as 'El Caracol' (the Snail) – a name inspired by its spiral staircase which leads to the top of the construction, from where it is believed that the Maya studied the solar system and made their astronomical calculations. There is evidence that, some time before the birth of Christ, they had perfected a calendar which was more accurate than the one we use today. Other important buildings are the Nunnery, the Iglesia church and the Casa Colarada (colored house).

About 3 miles (5 km) east of Chichén Itzá, you can visit the **Balancanché Cave,** one of the most impressive in the Yucatán. The name means 'hidden throne'. The throne inside, which is formed by hundreds of stalactites and stalagmites, resembles a ceiba tree. Within the depths of the caves is a lake *cenote* surrounding an altar dedicated to the Toltec god, Tlaloc. Only suitable for young and healthy visitors. There are several attractive hacienda-style hotels near Chichén Itzá, although visitors should make sure of their accommodations by reserving a room in advance. Less expensive hotels can be found 26 miles (42 km) away in Valladolid but a day trip from Mérida is an excellent alternative. Communications: By car, you can travel 75 miles (120 km) from Merida in the west and 125 miles (200 km) from Cancún in the east or by bus from Mérida or Cancún. Flights to the ruins can also be arranged. *Mérida 75mi/102 km.*

Cozumel D10

Quintana Roo (pop. 12,000). The charm of the Caribbean island resort of Cozumel lies in its soft white sandy beaches, shaded by palm trees and in its crystal-clear turquoise seas. For visitors, this island is a paradise for swimming, scuba diving, snorkeling, fishing and every kind of water sport. Cozumel's international airport has enabled this previously little-known area to become a popular spot for a relaxing vacation. It lies some 12 miles (20 km) off the coast of the Yucatán Peninsula and its area measures approximately 28 × 11 miles (45 × 17 km). Most of the hotels are situated on the western side of the island where the best beaches and calmest waters are to be found.

The **Palancar Reef,** one of the largest in the world, is about 1 mile (1½ km) off the southern tip of the island. In the clear waters, you can see giant formations of coral. Huge deposits of rare black coral were discovered here by the famous underwater explorer, Jacques Cousteau. Deep sea fishing is excellent for white marlin, blue-fin tuna, sailfish, mackerel and others. You can obtain details of fishing expeditions and procedures from your hotel. It is important to check which fish or

San Francisco beach, Cozumel

coral you can legally take as penalties can be stiff. The pretty little lagoon of **Chancanab** is one of many with deep, clear waters, connected to the sea by subterranean channels. The Robinson Crusoe cruise to idyllic **San Francisco beach** in the south makes an enjoyable excursion. Cozumel was discovered by Spaniard, Juan de Grijalva in 1518, later visited by Cortés and was subsequently used as a beachfront for pirates. There are a few remnants of Mayan ruins scattered about the island but the terrain makes it quite difficult to reach them. The capital, **San Miguel,** appears full of life with a pleasant zócalo, shops, in which some items are duty-free, and lively restaurants. Here the way of life is very informal and relaxed and it is possible to feel like a castaway on an agreeable desert island.

Places to stay range from deluxe to medium. Communications: international flights to United States and Mexican cities; local flights to Cancún, Playa del Carmen, Tulum, Chichén Itzá, Mérida, Chetumal; ferry boats to Isla Mujeres and the mainland; hydrofoil to Cancún. *Mainland 12 mi/20 km.*

Isla Mujeres B10

Quintana Roo (pop. 6000). This tiny Caribbean island, only ½ mile (1 km) across and 5 miles (8 km) long, lies to the north of Cozumel and is easily accessible by ferry from the mainland. The Maya used this spot for their fertility rites and when the Spaniards arrived here in 1517 they found the island littered with female idols, which is why it became known as 'Island of Women'. Most of the streets are unpaved and there are not very many cars. The island can easily be explored on foot and the way of life is decidedly informal and relaxing. It especially appeals to younger people and the escapist who is not seeking sophistication. The swimming and snorkeling is unsurpassed. **El Garrafón,** south of the island, is a unique undersea coral garden where you can dive and swim among the sea turtles and thousands of varieties of tropical fish. **Los Cocos** beach near the town is particularly good. Interesting excursions: a boat trip to the **Caves of the Sleeping Sharks,** (Jacques Cousteau made the only known discovery of sharks sleeping in an underwater cave here some years ago and you can make special arrangements to visit the caves); a day trip to **Contoy Island** — a bird sanctuary off the Yucatán Peninsula's northeast tip, where you can see flamingos, pelicans, ducks and many other species. A sunken pirate ship, *El Dormitorio,* can be seen from a boat just off the south coast of Contoy Island. Lodgings are modest. Communications: air to Cozumel, Cancún, Chetumal; ferry boats to Cozumel and mainland. *Mainland 6 mi/ 10 km.*

Cocoteros beach, Isla Mujeres

Mérida　　　　　　　　　　　　　C5

Yucatán (pop. 270,000). State capital of Yucatán. The Spaniards were so impressed by the white clothes worn by residents and by the cleanliness of the city that they named it 'White City'. Built on the site of an old Indian town, it was founded by the Spaniard, Francisco Montejo in 1542. The family built up a thriving business based on the henequen plant and opened up trading links with the United States and Europe. Many of Mérida's beautiful buildings show a marked French influence. The lovely tree-lined boulevard, Paseo de Montejo, looks similar to a miniature Champs Élysées with elegant mansions showing traces of Spanish, French, Italian and New Orleans influence. It is a pleasant little city with most of its streets bearing numbers rather than names. The tempo is easy going and the friendly, smiling faces of the Yucatecans add to its charm. Its large attractive central plaza is overlooked by a very large and impressive cathedral which was completed in 1598. One of the most important buildings is the Palacio de Gobierno (Governor's Palace) with splendid murals by Pacheco and the Hall of History on the second floor. On the south side of the main square, the Casa de Montejo, which was built in 1549 as a residence for the famous Montejo family, has some fine furniture and antiques imported from Europe. El Mercado (the market) is a short distance to the south, consisting of a large complex of stalls, shops and booths, filled with a wide variety of colorful goods. The University of Yucatán, originally a Jesuit institution, runs summer courses in Spanish, archaeology and cultural appreciation. The little church of La Ermita has a collection of Mayan and Toltec sculptures beautifully displayed in an adjoining garden. Traveling by horse-drawn carriage, known as a *calesa* is a graceful way of visiting the town.

A few miles north of Mérida lie the ruins of **Dzibilchaltún.** Its name means 'the place where there is writing on the stone'. This large Mayan city has some impressive buildings with elaborate façades and on the eastern end of its causeway, the Temple of the Seven Dolls is of particular note. A ceremonial well nearby is known as the Cenote Xlacá.

There are flights to domestic and international destinations. Bus and rail travel are available. *Mexico City 938 mi/1510 km*

Progreso　　　　　　　　　　　　B5

Yucatán (pop. 30,000). Progreso is about 25 minutes travel by car from Mérida. As the nearest beach resort, Progreso is popular with residents from Mérida, many of whom have houses and villas there. Since 1871 it has been the chief port of entry and export for the Yucatán, but it does not have much to offer the tourist from abroad for whom the Caribbean beaches hold greater attractions.

Accommodations for the visitor are modest. Access to Progreso is gained by taking a bus or car from Mérida. *Mérida 21 mi/33 km.*

Municipal Palace, Mérida

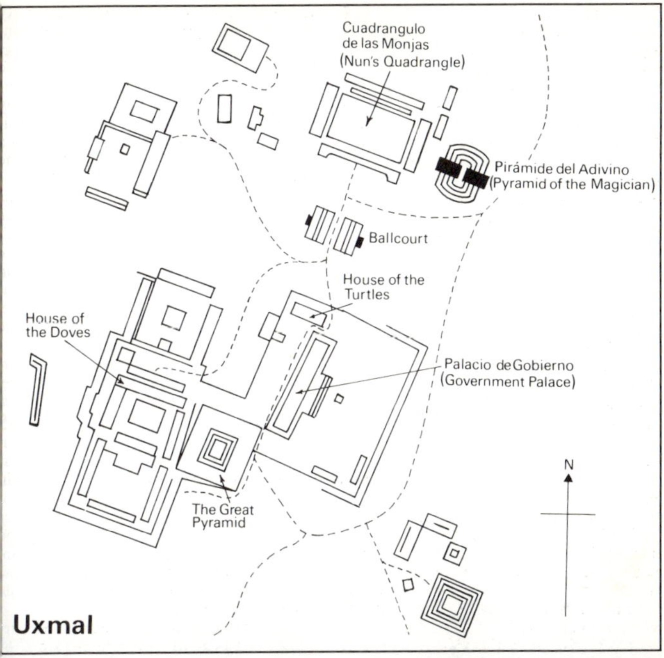

The Yucatán Peninsula 73

Uxmal is one of the most important of Mayan sites. The Pyramid of the Magician (above) contains interesting masks and mosaics

Uxmal D5

Yucatán. Uxmal lies about an hour's drive south of Mérida. The site is considerably smaller and less famous than Chichén Itzá but in many ways it is equally as significant. Uxmal was the major site of the Mayan classic period (AD 600—900). As the culture entered its postclassic phase and Chichén Itzá grew in importance, so Uxmal went into decline and finally lapsed into obscurity. This fine city with buildings of gleaming white limestone gilded by the sun, exudes a quiet elegance and beauty. Unlike Chichén Itzá, which bears strong evidence of the Toltec presence, Uxmal retained the simplicity of line created by the Mayan builders and is generally considered to be the best example of classic Mayan architecture.

The most prominent building is the Pirámide Del Adivino (Pyramid of the Magician) which consists of four stairways and a series of temples culminating in the highest with its large number of lattice designs. The climb to the top of the Pyramid is very steep but you are rewarded with a marvelous view of the site.

A short walk brings you to the graceful Mayan arch which gives entry to the delightful Cuadrángulo de Las Monjas (Nuns Quadrangle), a large square surrounded on all sides by rectangular buildings with carvings of *chacs* (rain gods), double-headed serpents etc. These buildings are widely admired for their symmetry, congruity and perfect proportions. Moving southward, the Palacio del Gobernador (Governor's Palace) is a spectacular construction. This long, rectangular building rests on a series of three terraces and has a façade composed of thousands of intricately carved stones, giving an impression of exquisite lacework. Other buildings of note are the Casa de las Tortugas (House of the Turtles), which is nearby, with its carvings of small turtles, el Cuadrángulo de las Palomas (House of the Doves), and la Pirámide Mayor (the Great Pyramid).

A light and sound show is held nightly, except for Mondays, with performances in Spanish and English. Pleasant hotels in the vicinity for overnight stays. *Mérida 47 mi/76 km.*

Sunset over the Gulf of Mexico, state of Campeche

Valladolid C8

Yucatán (pop. 25,000). The second largest city in the state of Yucatán. Valladolid is a convenient place to stop for lunch when you are traveling by road between Chichén Itzá and Cancún. The town was founded in the mid-16th century by the famous Montejo family. Its main feature is the San Bernardino Church in the suburb of Sisal — a fine example of Franciscan architecture. Near the town center there are two large *cenotes*, or wells — the Sis-ha and the Zaci. There is an open-air restaurant near the mouth of the Zaci. *Mérida 99 mi/160 km.*

THE WEST

This region, which includes states, Michoacán, Jalisco, and Colima, has a great deal to offer the visitor. Resorts such as Puerto Vallarta and hotel complexes such as Las Hadas are major tourist attractions along this beautiful coast. The region also has fine colonial towns, a rich folklore and culture and some of Mexico's most magnificent scenery in a climate ranging from temperate to tropical.

Michoacán, which lies to the west of Mexico City, is considered by some to be the most beautiful state in the country. A drive through this region with its scenic mountain roads and breathtaking curves is most rewarding. The alpine landscape and temperate climate are more reminiscent of Europe than of Mexico and the panorama is spectacular as you pass through the area of Mil Cumbres, the 'Thousand Peaks', on the approach to Pátzcuaro. There are beautiful lakes, rivers and waterfalls. Mexico's youngest volcano, Parícutin, erupted here in 1943 in the middle of a cornfield.

The neighboring state of Jalisco is characterized by wide open plains, cactus plantations and some wild, rugged country. It is the home of Lake Chapala, Mexico's largest lake, and a favorite retirement area for Americans in particular, who enjoy its near-perfect climate. Guadalajara, state capital and second largest city in Mexico, is an important commercial center. The mighty Sierra Madre range sweeps down Jalisco's western coast, forming high mountain peaks and deep gorges. The scenery is dramatic and this area is hot and tropical with lush, green vegetation.

The small state of Colima is hot and tropical by the coast and temperate at higher altitudes. Dominating this largely mountainous area with its great gorges and lush vegetation but just situated in Jalisco, are two majestic volcanoes, the Nevado de Colima and the Volcán de Colima, which has been active since 1957. You can sometimes see smoke belching from its crater.

All three states border the Pacific Ocean and the stretch of coast here is one of the loveliest in Mexico with numerous sandy beaches, bays and coves.

Michoacán has a great Indian heritage. It is the heartland of the Tarascan Indians, a proud and independent people who never succumbed to the neighboring Aztecs. In the 16th century, following the Spanish conquest of the Aztecs, the Tarascans suffered some years of cruel oppression under the Spaniard, Nuño de Guzmán. Happily, their fortunes changed for the better when he was replaced by the Spanish bishop, Vasco de Quiroga. This wise and humane man worked at giving assistance to the poor Indians who were barely surviving on fishing, farming and handicrafts. While learning from their culture he, in turn, helped them to become self-supporting by developing their skills and encouraging each village to specialize in its own particular craft. Affectionately known as 'Tata' (Father) Vasco, he was greatly loved by the Indians. The Tarascans retain a strong feeling for tradition and continue to earn their living as fishermen and craftsmen. Today the area is renowned as a great handidicraft center, producing beautiful lacquerware, finely carved chests, boxes and trays, ceramics and woven *sarapes* (blankets).

Jalisco was still primitive when the Spaniards arrived in the area but they encountered fierce opposition from the local inhabitants for a while. Finally having settled in the region, it was named 'Nueva Galicia' with Guadalajara as its capital. Real development began when the railroad arrived here from California several centuries later. Guadalajara has now grown into a thriving, modern metropolis. As a big industrial and agricultural center, Jalisco is one of Mexico's most important states but it is also rich in folklore and its costumes, songs and dances are among the most colorful in Mexico. The famous tequila is produced from the agave plant which grows in this region and Guadalajara's lively October festival is now becoming a worldwide attraction.

Early inhabitants of Colima are believed to have included the Nahua Indians around 500 BC and the Chichimecs around the 12th to 15th centuries. The culture of western Mexico did not reach the high levels of some other areas but

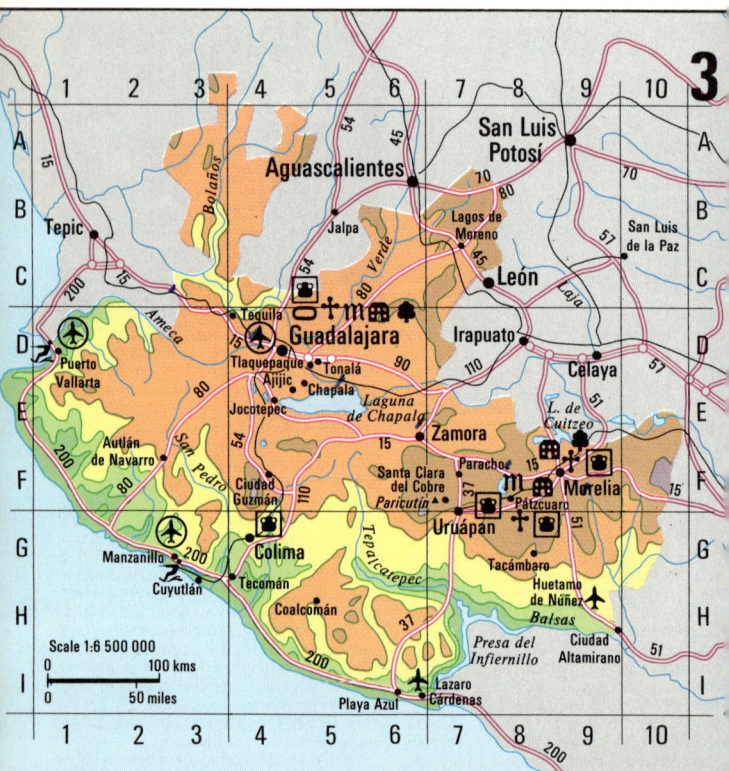

many interesting artifacts have been recovered. Large hollow clay figurines and vessels are common among the discoveries. Figures in Colima lack representation of deities, unlike most other Mexican cultures of the past.

It is said that, even before the arrival of the Spanish, Chinese junks would make occasional visits to the port of Manzanillo. The Spanish Conquistadores in the area built a fleet of galleons and in 1564 Captain Miguel López Legazpi led an expedition to conquer the Philippines for the Spanish crown. Trading links were firmly established with the Orient and a certain Chinese influence is still felt in the area. Isolated from the rest of the country in later years, the region became more accessible after a highway linked it with Jalisco in 1973.

Within the last decade, the increasing number of tourist developments along the coast has opened up the area. Main industries in western Mexico are agriculture, fruit, vegetables and grain, lemon-oil and copra, handicrafts, fishing and shipping, a thriving steel industry created by the giant steelworks at Lázaro Cárdenas in Michoacán and, of major importance, tourism.

The gastronomic speciality is seafood. A special delicacy is whitefish from Lake Pátzcuaro.

Festivals and events: Jan 15, regional dances and bullfights, Jocotepec (Jalisco); Feb, annual pilgrimage to San Juan de los Lagos (Jalisco); Late Feb or early March prior to Ash Wednesday, Manzanillo Carnival (Colima); May 5–10, Manzanillo May Festival — crowning of May Queen, songs and dancing (Colima); May 8, Founding of Manzanillo celebrations — floats, parades (Colima); Last week of May, Puerto Vallarta festival — parades, bullfights, fireworks, soccer (Jalisco); Oct 12, Columbus Day, Guadalajara (Jalisco); Oct 12, Celebration for the

Virgin of Zapopan, Guadalajara (Jalisco); throughout Oct, Guadalajara Festival — cultural events, concerts, ballet, opera, folk, sporting events (Jalisco); first week Nov, International Fishing Tournament — Puerto Vallarta (Jalisco); Nov, International Sailfish Tournament — Manzanillo (Colima); Nov 1—2, All Souls, All Saints — unique festival to honor the dead. All Night Wake by candlelight, Janitzio Island on Lake Pátzcuaro (Michoacán). In this ever-changing country, it is wise to check details of dates and times of events with the Mexican Tourist Office.

Ajijic E4
Jalisco. A pretty little town, with cobblestone streets, bordering Lake Chapala. The atmosphere in the town, which is full of boutiques and galleries, is informal and relaxing and it is popular with artists and writers. Posada Ajijic is a lovely old colonial inn on the shores of the lake and, with tropical gardens and a pool, it is pleasant for a weekend stay. *Guadalajara 39 mi/ 63 km.*

Chapala E5
Jalisco (pop. 16,000). Resort town on the northern shore of Lake Chapala. Founded in the sixteenth century, its name is derived from Chapalah, chief of the Taltica Indians who inhabited the area before the colonial era. Here, in the villa on Zaragoza Street, D.H. Lawrence wrote *The Plumed Serpent*.

On the pleasant waterfront, which has bars and restaurants, there are serenading *mariachis* who charge for each song but you should always bargain with them! Launches can be rented for a trip on the lake. The perfect climate and easy way of life here have attracted many foreign settlers, especially Americans, who have homes along the lakeside. *Guadalajara 31 mi/50 km.*

Colima G4
Colima (pop. 125,000). State capital, about two hour's drive inland from Manzanillo. The town was founded in the early 16th century by the Spanish and has two museums of note: the Museum of Western Mexico Indian Culture which houses a large and interesting collection of regional archaeological finds and there is a fascinating museum of antique cars. *Guadalajara 165 mi/265 km.*

Guadalajara D5
Jalisco (pop. 2,200,000). State capital and second largest city in Mexico, Guadalajara is a fast-developing commercial center, which successfully combines the old with the new. It is built on a mile-high plain, surrounded by wild, jungle terrain and has one of the best climates in Mexico with mild, clear days most of the year round. This is a city of large squares, lovely parks, flower-lined boulevards and fine colonial churches. The colonial buildings blend in tastefully with 20th-century skyscrapers and pleasant suburban residential areas offer good facilities for modern living. General Nuño de Guzmán founded the city. It was his ambition to make it capital of the kingdom of Nueva Galicia and create an independent state. Although this never materialized, Guadalajara did maintain a measure of political and judicial autonomy during the colonial period. It began to prosper during this time and much of its wealth was put into the construction of this fine city but real growth only properly started following the advent of the railroad in the late 19th century.

The center consists of four main plazas in the shape of a cross: the Plaza de Armas with its bandstand, the Plaza de la Liberación with its monument to the heroes of the Mexican Revolution, the Plaza de la Rotunda and Plaza Laureles with foun-

Statue of Cuauhtémoc, Guadalajara

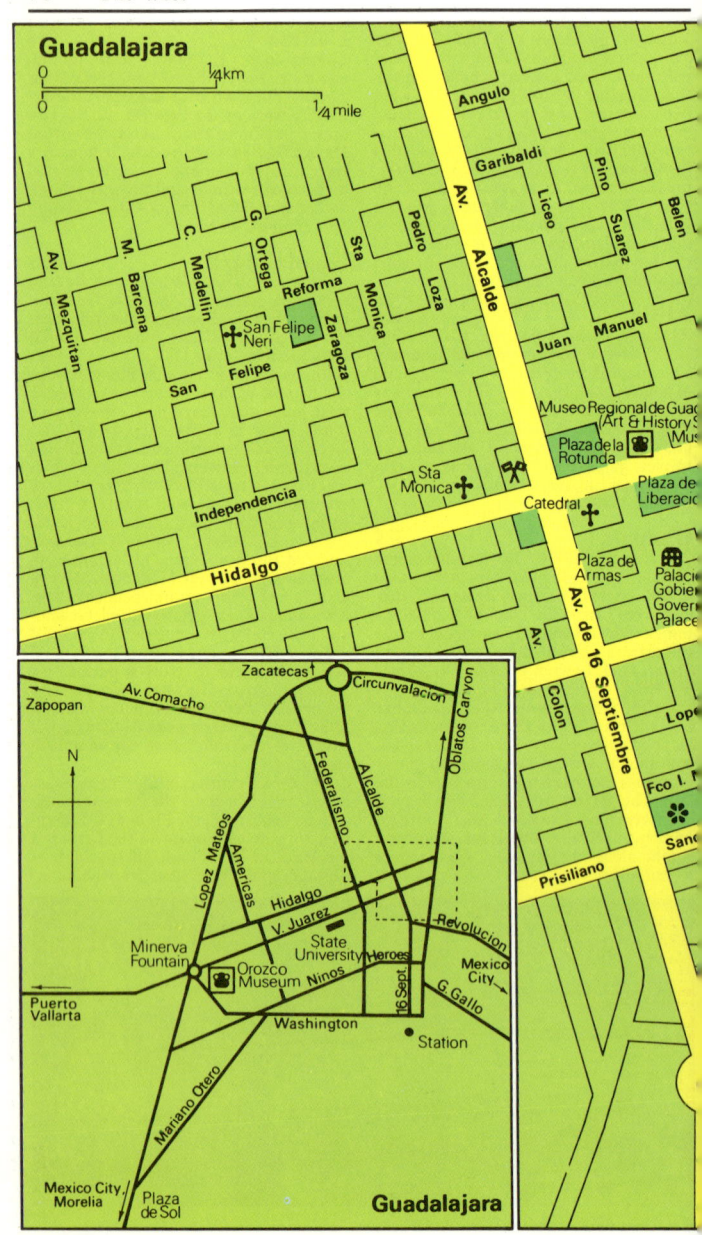

tains, shady trees and flowers. The main cathedral, overlooking this spacious area, is Guadalajara's pride and glory. Started in the 16th century, several styles can be recognized in its structure including Gothic, Baroque and Renaissance, with magnificent twin towers of Byzantine architecture. The Palacio de Gobierno (Government Palace), facing the Plaza de Armas, has some fine murals by José Clemente Orozco who lived from 1883 to 1949. He is rated as one of Mexico's finest muralists and performed much of his work in Guadalajara. The Teatro Degollado, off Plaza de la Liberación, is a beautiful building in Greek style. As the city's foremost cultural center, it has year-round performances of ballet and concerts as well as folk shows. The Museo Regional de Guadalajara (art and history state museum), on Plaza de la Rotunda, is worth a visit. To the east, across the Calzada Independencia, lies the Hospicio Cabañas. This former orphanage has now been converted to a cultural center built around an attractive series of patios. Orozco's mural, *Four Horsemen of the Apocalypse* which can be found here, is regarded as a masterpiece. The state university, west of the downtown area, is a fine building dating back to the 1920s and this too, has some splendid Orozco murals. Colorful folkloric performances are staged here.

Horse-drawn carriages line up by the Plaza de Armas to take you on a sightseeing tour of the city. It is worth stopping by the Mercado Libértad, the largest market in this part of Mexico. The place to relax here is the Plazuela de los Mariachis. Guadalajara is the home of the *mariachis* —lively musicians who played at weddings during the French occupation of Mexico in the latter half of the 19th century. The name *mariachi* is derived from the French *mariage* (marriage). It is pleasant to linger in the square named after them and to hear them play.

Guadalajara has several fine golf clubs and tennis courts. The impressive soccer stadium, Estadio Jalisco, was built for use in the 1970 and 1986 World Cup soccer championships. There are bullfights on Sundays.

You should not miss the opportunity to visit **Tlaquepaque** 5 miles (8 km) to the east, which is one of Mexico's most famous art and craft centers. This pretty little village is crammed with boutiques and arcades laden with a large variety of colorful handicrafts produced in the region. Here you can watch skilled potters, glass blowers, weavers and other craftsmen at work.

Tonala, which lies 7 miles (11 km) east of Tlaquepaque, is famed for its ceramics, papier-mâché and glassware. *Mexico City 364 mi/586 km.*

Jocotepec   E4
Jalisco. This attractive little fishing village is at the extreme end of Lake Chapala's western shores. It provides a charmingly rustic refuge for artists and writers. Noted for its fine *sarapes* (blankets). *Guadalajara 34 mi/55 km.*

Manzanillo   G3
Colima (pop. 55,000). Manzanillo is situated on a narrow Isthmus between the Pacific Ocean and Cuyutlán Lagoon. Cortés named it after the camomile (Spanish: manzanilla) which adorned the town and he chose it as his place of retirement. It became an important seaport when the Spanish settlers started sailing from Manzanillo to other continents. The Philippine Islands were discovered during the course of their voyages and oriental influences linger in these parts.

The town is Mexico's most important west coast port and is a world-renowned sailfish center. Deep-sea fishing expeditions can be organized for enthusiasts. While the city itself holds no great attractions for the tourist, its setting is beautiful with the magnificent sweep of mountains down to the coast. Its chief appeal lies in the sandy beaches which stretch northward to Puerto Vallarta and the lush green vegetation of its hinterland.

Manzanillo airport now serves as an important gateway to the string of hotels dotted along the coastline. The hotel complex, Las Hadas (the fairies), lies about 30 minutes from the airport. It was built by the Bolivian millionaire, Antenor Patiño, and is one of Mexico's most unusual hotels. Dazzling white domes and towers, winding cobblestone streets and archways give it the appearance of some fantasy Moorish village. Set in its own bay, this extensive complex has a sandy beach, marina and lagoon-type pool in lush tropical gardens. Throughout the year it forms a splash of color with an abundance of flowers in striking shades of scarlet, pink, purple and orange. Quaint little electric cars provide transportation around the complex. The more recently built holiday village, Club Maeva, with Mediterranean-style villas is nearby.

Further up the coast, 47 miles (56 km) from the airport lies the romantic hotel complex of Hotel Plaza Careyes which is quite different in character from Las Hadas. It is built hacienda-style in soft, sandcolored stone and surrounds a lovely little palm-fringed bay. The hotel is somewhat isolated and it makes an ideal spot for a completely relaxing holiday.

There is a good surfing beach at **Cuyutlán**, some 30 miles (48 km) from Manzanillo. In spring you can witness the amazing spectacle of the *ola verde:* a huge green wave full of marine vegetation which comes crashing down onto the shores. *Guadalajara 217 mi/349 km.*

Morelia F9
Michoacán (pop. 300,000). State capital and a university city. Morelia is considered the 'aristocrat' of all Mexico's colonial cities, with beautiful churches, palaces and buildings of rose-colored stone. It was founded in the 16th century by Antonio de Mendoza, first Viceroy of New Spain, and named Valladolid. In 1828 the name was changed to Morelia in honor of José Maria Morelos, one of Mexico's great patriots during the Independence wars against the Spanish. With few modern buildings, Morelia has been maintained in the traditions of the colonial era.

In the center of town, the Plaza de los Martires (also known as the Plaza de Armas) is an attractive square surrounded by graceful arcades and sidewalk cafés. To one side the cathedral, dating back to the 17th century, has a beautiful rose stone façade and its 200 ft tower is considered to be one of the finest examples of Plateresque architecture. The 18th-century church of Santa Rosa, at the intersection of Nigromante and Santiago Tadia, is also worth exploring.

Other buildings of interest: in the west of the city, the Colegio de San Nicolas, founded in 1540 and the second oldest educational institution in the Americas; the centrally situated Baroque-style Palacio de Gobierno (Governor's Palace), with a splendid mural by the Michoacán artist, Alfredo Zalce; in the south of the city, the Casa de Morelos, which was the home of Morelos is now a museum with interesting historical manuscripts. The city has lovely gardens, trees and flowers and a pleasant climate. It is not overrun by tourists and exudes an air of quiet grace and elegance. Attractive handicrafts can be bought from the arcade shops and good buys are lacquerware, pottery, copperware and wood carvings.

East of Morelia, the huge **aqueduct** built in 1785 to transport water to the town from nearby springs is an impressive landmark. There are a few resort hotels in the nearby **hills of Santa Maria** from where you have a good view of graceful Morelia. *Mexico City 193 mi/310 km.*

Pátzcuaro F8
Michoacán (pop. 30,000). A rustic little town near Lake Pátzcuaro. As the home of the Tarascan Indians, it has kept its distinctive flavor. It has charming red-tiled houses, tiny cobblestone streets and attracts artists and photographers. Horses and donkeys provide transportation and cars are not commonly used.

Butterfly net fishing on Lake Pátzcuaro

In the 16th century the local inhabitants suffered cruel Spanish oppression until the arrival of Bishop Vasco de Quiroga in 1540. This wise and compassionate man devoted himself to helping the poor Indians to support themselves by developing their trades. Little has changed over the years and the Tarascans continue to earn their livelihood by fishing, farming and handicrafts. Buildings of note are the Basilica de Nuestra Señora de la Salud; the church of San Agustin, now known as la Biblioteca (library), with a Juan O'Gorman mural depicting the history of this area; the Casa del Gigante (House of the Giant), which is a former colonial palace with a huge warrior carved on one of its pillars; the Casa de los Once Patios (House of Eleven Patios), formerly a convent and now a crafts and information center. The Museo de Artes Populares (museum of popular arts) also has a fine collection of handicrafts and ceramics.

About 2½ miles (4 km) north of the town, **Lake Pátzcuaro** is one of the highest lakes in Mexico. On some fiesta days the local fishermen bring out their unique 'butterfly nets', a wonderful subject for budding photographers. Lakeside restaurants serve the whitefish from the lake, considered a delicacy throughout Mexico.

Janitzio Island on Lake Pátzcuaro

Boat trips go to **Janitzio,** the largest of the islands, where quaint little houses of all colors rise up a steep hill crowned by an enormous statue of Morelos, hero of Independence. Any visitor to Janitzio on the first of November should not miss the opportunity to witness the unique festival, the Day of the Dead, held there. The villagers decorate the graves of their departed ones with flowers and offer baskets of food. The area is lit up by thousands of candles during the nightlong wake.

You can also visit the smaller islands of **Yunuén, Jarácuaro, La Pacanda** and **Tecuén**. Jarácuaro, which can also be reached by causeway from the mainland, is a major producer of the famous Mexican sombrero. *Mexico City 227 mi/365 km.*

Playa Azul   I6
Michoacán (pop. 3000). Playa Azul is Michoacán's only resort. It offers good fishing but is otherwise unremarkable. Down the coast, the giant steelworks of Las Truchas is one of the largest in Latin America. **Lázaro Cárdenas,** nearby, has encountered a rapid growth in population and is fast developing into a dynamic boom town. *Mexico City 430 mi/698 km.*

Puerto Vallarta   D1
Jalisco (pop. 60,000). Puerto Vallarta is one of Jalisco's major tourist attractions and one of Mexico's most popular resorts. It lies in the beautiful Bay of Banderas, surrounded by a ring of mountains and covered with rich tropical foliage. Its sandy beaches are superb. Until the mid-1950s or so Puerto Vallarta was an unknown and little frequented fishing village. Gradually a few modest hotels appeared and an air service was established linking it with Guadalajara. It was the filming of *Night of the Iguana* with Richard Burton in the early 1960s and all the resulting publicity the film stars attracted which really put the area on the map.

Puerto Vallarta

Puerto Vallarta has now developed into a modern, swinging resort with a wide range of hotels offering all facilities. There is always plenty to do on the beaches during the day and all types of water sports are available. The range of activities includes waterskiing, sailboarding, parasailing, fishing and donkey polo on the beach as well as tennis and golf. The center of town retains its old picturesque charm as little groups of donkeys with their loads amble up its steep, winding cobblestone streets. The resort has a certain Bohemian appeal for artists and film people, some of whom have villas tucked away in the hills. Puerto Vallarta is renowned for its spectacular sunsets and evenings are lively with a good choice of restaurants, bars and discos.

You can take a boat trip to **Mismaloya beach** (scene of the filming) for a picnic, good swimming and fishing, or to Yelapa,

Condominiums at Puerto Vallarta

Uruápan G7

Michoacán (pop. 100,000). Uruápan is a pleasant little semitropical town set in magnificent surrounding countryside. The Tarascan meaning of the name is 'place where the flowers bloom'. Museo Regional de Arte Popular, on Plaza Morelos, is a small museum with an excellent collection of Uruápan lacquerware as well as displays of pottery and crafts from all over Michoacán.

About 7 miles (11 km) away from Uruápan traveling southward, you can visit the spectacular **Tzaráracua waterfall** which has a magnificent cascade of gushing water and a permanent rainbow. The volcano, **Paricutin,** which erupted in 1943 is nearby. It was active for some years and caused destruction in the area. **Santa Clara del Cobra** is well-known for its copperware and, also in the vicinity, the town of **Paracho** is renowned for violin and guitar making. *Mexico City 264 mi/425 km.*

a wild jungle beach surrounded by mountains. A further trip in small canoes takes you across the bay and a short walk in the jungle leads you to a hidden waterfall where you can take a refreshing dip in its natural pool. **Yelapa** has a tiny hotel and restaurant on the beach and you can always sample a few days primitive existence in this lovely remote spot. *Guadalajara 203 mi/327 km.*

Tequila D4

Jalisco (pop. 12,000). Mexico's famous fiery drink, tequila, is produced here and takes its name from the town. The families of Sauza and Cuervo are the two major producers of tequila, which was first distilled here in 1600. There are 24 distilleries and guided tours are available showing how the drink is made, from the extraction of the juice from the heart of the *agave tequiliana* plant through to the processes of fermentation and distillation. *Guadalajara 32 mi/52 km.*

Little girl learning to cook

CENTRAL MEXICO

The seven states included in this section (Guanajuato, Hidalgo, Puebla, Querétaro, México, Morelos and Tlaxcala) form a large area which encircles the capital, Mexico City. It is the most heavily populated region of Mexico and is of major economic importance as well as being attractive to tourists. The variations of climate range from the *tierras frias* (cold lands), with altitudes of over 6000 ft (18030 m), to the *tierras templadas* (temperate lands), with altitudes averaging 4000 ft (1200 m). Most of the larger cities are built on the high plateau and come within the zone of the *tierras frías*. The term 'cold lands' is somewhat deceptive since the days are normally warm and sunny — temperatures drop from cool to cold only when the sun goes down. Even at these high altitudes, there is color, blossom and greenery throughout the year. The *tierras templadas* have an ideal, spring-like climate. Within this area lie vast expanses of pine forests, rolling hills and valleys. high mountains and wide plains. Some of the scenery is quite spectacular. There are also lakes and rivers, with some fine National Parks in magnificent surroundings.

To the south, the landscape is dominated by beautiful snow-capped volcanoes. Mexico's highest peak, Pico de Orizaba or 'Morning Star' (located in Veracruz state), rises majestically to an altitude of 18,700 ft (5700 m) and is perpetually snow-covered. The Nevado de Toluca, towering over the state of Mexico, is also covered with snow most of the year round but the most famous and perhaps the most impressive are the twin volcanoes Popocatépetl (known as Popo for short) and Ixtaccihuatl. Their beautiful snow-capped peaks were once visible from the capital. Sadly, growth and pollution have taken their toll and now they can only be glimpsed on a clear day. Popo, 17,887 ft (5452 m), is known as the Smoking Mountain and Ixtaccíhuatl, 17,342 ft (5286 m), as the Sleeping Woman. According to Aztec mythology, Popo was a brave warrior who fell in love with an Indian princess. When she heard, mistakenly, that he had been killed in battle, she died from a broken heart. Popo was grief stricken when he returned and the two lovers were turned into volcanoes to be united forever.

The Aztecs, who started settling in the area around the 14th century, built up a great empire, exercising enormous power and influence over a very large area until their defeat at the hands of the Spanish Conquistadores in 1521. There followed 300 years of colonial rule during which period many beautiful towns with fine churches and palaces were built by the Spanish. Most of the best examples are to be found in the Central Highlands.

Early in the 19th century, the Independence movement started to take shape and it was in the state of Guanajuato, known as the Cradle of Independence, that the conspirators plotted the first stages of the struggle for their freedom. In 1810, a parish priest, Father Miguel Hidalgo rang the church bell from the little town of Dolores and rallied the people to take up arms against Spanish oppression. Major battles were fought in the states of Guanajuato and Querétaro. The two great leaders of the Mexican movement, Hidalgo and Ignacio Allende, were captured and executed within the first year of the war but, when the Mexicans gained their independence in 1821, the names of the towns of their birth were adapted to Dolores Hidalgo and San Miguel de Allende in their honor.

The century following Independence was a period of chaos and political upheaval. In 1864, in a bid to take over Mexico, the French installed Maximilian of Austria as Emperor. The most famous monument to his brief reign is Paseo de la Reforma (modeled on the Champs Élysées in Paris) in Mexico City. In 1867 he was captured and executed by the Juárist Mexicans on the Hill of Bells overlooking Querétaro. Today there is a chapel marking the spot, built by the Mexican government.

There was an uprising of the poor against the rich in the Mexican Revolution of 1910. The state of Morelos was a battleground for one of its most prominent leaders, Emiliano Zapata who was born in the area. Zapata was an idealist with a real desire to obtain justice for the poor peas-

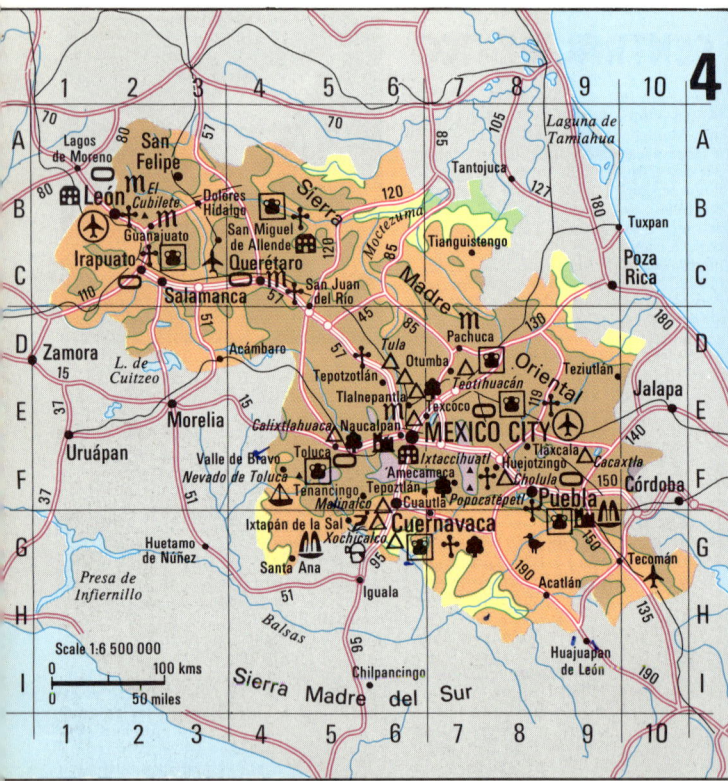

ants who worked the land. With his band of followers he made constant attacks on the rich estates, burning crops and causing much devastation. He later joined forces with that other great leader of the Revolution, the notorious Pancho Villa, but Zapata was betrayed and shot in 1919. As a fighter in the cause for the redistribution of land, he has ever since been revered as one of Mexico's great heroes.

The state of México is rich in archaeological sites, ranging from numerous small sites and isolated pyramids scattered about the countryside to the grandeur of the Sun and Moon pyramids at Teotihuacán. Mexico's finest colonial towns are located in the central region and there are many vacation centers and spa resorts. The area offers popular weekend retreats for Mexican nationals and tourists.

An economy based on a variety of thriving industries makes the area one of the richest in Mexico. Agriculture, cattle, handicrafts and tourism also make their contribution and wine is produced in Querétaro and Hidalgo.

Gastronomic specialities: *Mole poblano* is one of Mexico's most famous dishes. Allegedly created by nuns in Puebla, this is a rich sauce consisting of many spices, chillies and unsweetened chocolate. It is often prepared on feast days and special occasions and is used as an accompaniment for turkey, pork or chicken. *Chiles en nogada* are stuffed green chillies, topped with a white sauce of ground walnuts, cream cheese and red pomegranate seeds, all of which combine the red, white and green of the Mexican flag. Querétaro produces a spicy pork sausage, *chorizo*, and a very sweet dessert, *Cajeta*, made from goat's milk.

Festivals and events: Jan 20, festival in honor of Independence hero Allende, San Miguel de Allende (Guanajuato); Mar 3, local fiesta Amecameca (México); May

3, colorful fiestas in Valle de Bravo (México) and Ixtapán de la Sal (México); May 5, Battle of Puebla. National Day; throughout May, Puebla Fair (Puebla); Feb or Mar (shortly before Lent). Colorful carnival in Tepoztlán (Morelos) and Huejotzingo (Puebla); Mid July, fiestas in Querétaro; Aug 15—16, Annual Fair; handicrafts, streets paved with flowers Huamantla (Tlaxcala); Sept 14, Toluca fair and fiesta (México); Dec 12, fiesta Valle de Bravo (México). In this ever-changing country, it is wise to check details of dates and times of events with the Mexican Tourist Office.

Cuautla   G7
Morelos (pop. 25,000). Second city of Morelos and home of the revolutionary leader Emiliano Zapata. Popular weekend spa resort with a spectacular view of the volcanoes, Popocatépetl and Ixtaccíhuatl.

A short distance from Cuautla, the attractive Hacienda Cocoyoc hotel offers horseback riding, golf, swimming and tennis, set in lovely gardens surrounded by fields and woods.

Oaxtepec, formerly the site of Aztec king Montezuma's botanical gardens, is a popular recreational spot, with swimming pools and playgrounds. *Mexico City 72 mi/ 115 km.*

Cuernavaca   F6
Morelos (pop. 600,000). Cuernavaca, which is the capital of Morelos, has the perfect climate, earning it the name 'City of Eternal Spring'. This, together with its proximity to Mexico City (about one hour's drive), has long made it a favorite retreat for people from the capital. The Aztecs used Cuernavaca for its thermally heated springs and mineral waters and

Diego Rivera mural depicting the conquest of Mexico, Cuernavaca

today many Mexicans have beautiful weekend homes here with lovely gardens and swimming pools. Buildings of interest: the Palacio de Cortés, which was built in 1530 and once housed state government offices, is now a museum with fine Diego Rivera murals; a fortified Franciscan church, a short distance southwest of the center, which was founded in the 16th century and is one of the oldest cathedrals in Mexico; the 18th-century Borda Gardens nearby, created by José de la Borda who made his fortune from silver mining. Not far east of the downtown area, **Chapultepec Park** is an attractive recreational area with pools, playground and a miniature railway. The Aztec pyramid, **Teopanzolco** lies about a mile to the northeast of the town center.

The ruins of **Xochicalco,** which means 'House of the Flowers', lies about an hour's drive to the southwest of Cuernavaca and this hilltop ancient city is believed by archaeologists to be of great significance to our understanding of ancient Mexican cultures. A short distance to the northeast of Cuernavaca, the little Indian village of **Tepoztlán** is situated, where *Nahuatl*, the ancient language of the Aztecs, is still spoken. The village is perched dramatically on a clifftop and can only be reached on foot. A steep climb up narrow winding streets takes you to the shrine of Tepozteco dedicated to Tepoztecatl (god of pulque, the fermented sap of the maguey plant) where there is a magnificent view of the surrounding countryside. West of Cuernavaca, near the border with Guerrero state, the impressive **Cacahuamilpa Caves** have a wonderful array of stalactites, stalagmites and arches. Guided tours are available.

About 30 minutes' drive southeast from town lies the resort area of **Lake Tequesquitengo,** where you can swim, water-ski and go horseback riding. Lakeside restaurants serve fresh seafood. Nearby is the Hacienda Vista Hermosa, converted from an old sugar-mill hacienda into an attractive hotel with lovely gardens and an ancient aqueduct over the swimming pool. The small village of **Malinalco,** just over the border in México state, has an impressive circular temple with fine sculptures carved out of the rock. This was the final refuge of the Aztec priests who were hunted by the Spanish Conquistadores. *Mexico City 53 mi/85 km.*

Dolores Hidalgo B3
Guanajuato (pop. 22,000). This little town's main interest is historical. It was here that the first step was taken towards independence from the Spanish when Father Miguel Hidalgo rang the bell of the parish church on the night of September 16, 1810, summoning the people to take up arms and fight for their freedom. Their celebrated cry for freedom, *el grito* is re-enacted every year, when throughout Mexico on this date, they ceremoniously ring the bell. *Mexico City 230 mi/370 km.*

Guanajuato B2
Guanajuato (pop. 50,000). Guanajuato (Hill of Frogs) is about four hours' drive north of Mexico City. It is one of Mexico's most beautifully preserved colonial towns, nestling in a valley surrounded by a ring of mountains in a spectacular setting. The town has little squares, stone steps and narrow cobblestone streets, so narrow that one has been named the *Calle del Beso* (Street of the Kiss) as it is reckoned that a kiss could be exchanged between two people leaning out of their respective balconies. Houses are painted in all colors — blue, pink, yellow. A feature of Guanajuato is its underground street which follows the bed of the river that once flowed through the town. Guanajuato was once one of the country's most important mining towns and, in the 1700s particularly, it was one of the world's largest producers of silver. When the Independence Wars began, Guanajuato was the first major city to be taken by the Mexicans. A simple local miner known as El Pipila set fire to the Alhóndiga de Granaditas (granary) where the Spaniards had taken refuge from the advancing armies. El Pipila lost his own

The Juárez Theater hosts many events including international opera and dance, Guanajuato

life in the process and became one of the great heroes of the movement. A gigantic statue of him stands on a nearby hilltop overlooking the city. The following year the two great Independence leaders, Hidalgo and Allende, were among those captured and killed by the Spanish. Their heads remained on display in the granary until the end of the wars as an example to the rebels. Today, the Alhóndiga, which can be found on Positos, is a museum to the town's history.

Guanajuato's university is one of the most important in Mexico. This former Jesuit school became a state university in 1945 and courses are taught in both Spanish and English. The Diego Rivera museum, at no. 47 Positos, was the birthplace of this famous muralist. It is now a center for art shows, lectures and cultural events and some of Rivera's paintings and sketches can be seen here.

About 1 mile (1½ km) along Calzada del Pantéon you can find the **Pantéon** which has an interesting, if gruesome collection of well-preserved mummies. The old Church of **La Valenciana** stands 2½ miles (4 km) along Dolores Hidalgo Road, alongside the disused Valenciana silver mine which was once one of the most profitable mines in Mexico.

The International Cervantes Festival staged here, for two or three weeks at the end of April, has now become a world-wide attraction, but there is a possibility that the dates will be moved to the Fall and it is wise to check with the tourist board. Theater companies from all over the world join in with the local *estudiantinas* (student minstrels from the university). There are outdoor concerts, operas and dances and the works of Cervantes are staged against the perfect backdrop of this delightful little town.

A short trip up into the mountains of **El Cubilete** (the dicebox) takes you to the statue of the **Cristo Rey** (Christ the King) stretching out his arms to bless the valley below. The view of surrounding mountains, rich farmlands and lakes is magnificent and marks the geographical center of Mexico. *Mexico City 227 mi/365 km.*

Irapuato   C2
Guanajuato (pop. 110,000). Colonial city known for its important strawberry-growing industry. Buildings of note: Palacio Municipal; Templo de San Francisco with paintings by Mexican artist Miguel Cabrera; large football stadium used as a World Cup venue. Limited accommodations. *Mexico City 200 mi/321 km.*

León   B2
Guanajuato (pop. 624,816). This lively, booming commercial center is renowned as a major producer of shoes and leather goods. It has a pleasant main square and fine colonial buildings. Of special interest are the Palacio Municipal (City Hall), the cathedral of Nuestra Señora de la Luz on the main square and the little church of Nuestra Señora de los Angeles, with some catacombs and exquisite carvings. León is very sports-minded and has a large football stadium, Estadio Nou Camp, for use in the 1986 World Cup and by two professional soccer teams. *Mexico City 234 mi/376 km.*

Pachuca   D7
Hidalgo (pop. 150,000). Pachuca is the capital of the state of Hidalgo and it was founded in the 16th century on the site of an Otomi Indian village which was under Aztec rule. A striking feature of the town is the huge statue of Emiliano Zapata which you will see at the entrance. The Palacio de Gobierno (Governor's Palace) has an interesting mural by Jesús Becerril depicting the liberation of mankind. *Mexico City 56 mi/90 km.*

Puebla   F8
Puebla (pop. 532,00). Capital of Puebla state, and fourth largest city in Mexico. According to legend, a bishop from the neighboring town of Tlaxcala had a vision of two angels laying out a city in a beautiful spot surrounded by trees, flowers and tall volcanic peaks. The place he found was the site upon which Puebla was built and the city became known as 'City of Angels'. Its setting is magnificent. Situated in a valley, crowned by three of Mexico's most majestic volcanoes, *Popocatépetl, Ixtaccíhuatl* and *Pico de Orizaba.* Artisans from the Talavera region of their native land were among the first Spanish settlers in the area in the 16th century and tilemaking soon became a flourishing industry. Practically all of Puebla's churches, houses and Spanish patios have been decorated with Talavera tiles from this period. Puebla has often been the the center of events in Mexico's history. The occupying French troops were defeated there by the Mexicans on May 5 1862 and this date, commemorated every year, is one of Mexico's major National Days.

The town was neatly and carefully laid out. It has a large central zócalo with tropical flowers, trees and a bandstand surrounded by arcades and the cathedral on its eastern side is one of the largest in the country. The cathedral was completed in the 17th century and has a lovely altar of onyx and marble and an impressive façade. Nearby, the Chapel of the Rosary in Santo Domingo church, is noted for its

Central Mexico

Popocatépetl

beautiful decorations. It has a jeweled statue of the Virgin Mary on the altar and walls decorated with carvings and sculptures. The Santa Rosa Convent, in the north of the city, is said to be where the nuns concocted the famous *mole poblano* dish. The convent is now a museum with a well-preserved kitchen, which has been decorated with Talavera tiles. The secret convent of Santa Monica, nearby, is an interesting building historically, which operated undercover when the Mexican Reform Laws of 1857 abolished convents. It has hidden passages and doors and remained undiscovered until 1934.

The convent is now a museum containing religious paintings and relics. Buildings of interest near the zócalo are the Bello museum; the Palafox library, which has a good collection of rare books; the state university; to the east, the Casa del Alfeñique (regional museum) which has a good collection of archaeological exhibits. The restored Forts of Loreto and Guadalupe (site of the Battle of Puebla in 1862) are also worth visiting. Puebla's most important sporting stadium is the Estadio Cuauhtémoc which is used for World Cup soccer matches.

Cholula, about 9 miles (15 km) west of Puebla, is reputed to have over 365 churches. In recent years archaeologists made a great discovery when they uncovered the pyramid of Tepanapa. This turned out to be the largest in the world, even larger than the mighty pyramid of Cheops in Egypt. Although much remains to be done, excavations have so far revealed miles of tunnel inside and, throughout the centuries of its use, structures were built, one on top of the other. It is believed that Cholula was a great religious center for many centuries. The Spanish-built church of Nuestra Señora de los Remedios was built on top of the pyramid and provides an excellent view of the area.

Church of San Francisco Acatepec, Cholula

Southeast of Puebla is the spa town of **Tehuacán,** where the famous Tehuacán mineral water is bottled and distributed.

A large **wild game reserve** which is the only one of its kind in Mexico, with lions, tigers, elephants, giraffes and many more species of animals and birds lies about 25 minutes drive south of Puebla.

A drive northwest of Puebla takes you to Amecameca, noted for its ceramics. Beyond this, a road leads through the pine forests of Ixtaccíhuatl/Popocatépetl Park. This leads to Tlamacas (known as **Cortés Pass**) which is the spot Cortés passed through on his way from Veracruz to the ancient capital of Tenochtitlán and the ultimate conquest of Mexico. From here you have a magnificent view of the twin volcanoes, 'Popo', the warrior, standing guard over the recumbent Ixtaccíhuatl. The scenery all around is alpine, fresh and green. From here experienced climbers may set out to conquer the icy summits. *Mexico City 78 mi/126 km.*

Querétaro C4

Querétaro (pop. 200,000). State capital. This is one of Mexico's most historic cities with magnificent churches, splendid palaces and attractive plazas. The Aztecs originally used the site as an outpost but it was conquered by the Spanish and they then founded the city of Querétaro in 1531 in its place. In the early 1800s Querétaro was the scene of fierce fighting at the beginning of the struggle for independence from the Spanish. It was here that Emperor Maximilian, after three short years of reign, took refuge from the advancing troops of Benito Juárez. Maximilian was betrayed, captured and, in June 1867, he was executed by a firing squad on the Hill of Bells overlooking the city. The spot where Maximilian was executed is commemorated by a small chapel near the summit, erected by the Austrian government. Alongside is a gigantic statue of Benito Juárez, the man who overthrew him and went on to become one of Mexico's most prominent Presidents. Mexico's Constitution was written and signed here in 1917.

Querétaro, which was once a leading center for the opals mined in the region, has a tradition of industry including furniture-making and today it is an important commercial center with huge manufacturing plants. Because its industrialized outskirts are not particularly inviting, Querétaro is often bypassed by those traveling north from Mexico City, but a visit to the center will reveal a truly beautiful city — orderly, neat and very Spanish in character.

A distinguishing landmark, visible from quite a distance, is the 5 mile (8 km) long aqueduct with 30 ft (9 m) high arches. It is a remarkable feat of 18th-century Spanish engineering. Among Querétaro's many churches, the following are worth visiting: the 18th-century church of Santa Rosa de Viterbo, southwest of the center, with two enormous flying buttresses; the church of San Felipe Neri, completed in 1804. It overlooks the Plaza de la Constitución and has an ornate exterior with an unusually plain interior; the church of Santa María de Guadalupe, on Paseo de la Corregidora and Pasteur Norte with elaborate organ pipes and twin towers which are topped with wrought-iron crosses and red, white and green tile decoration; the Church and Convent of the Cross at Plaza Venustiano Carranza which was the center of operations for a Franciscan order.

The Plaza de Toros Santa María is one of the most important bull rings in Mexico and the bullfights which take place there attract top fighters. The Estadio Municipal is used as a World Cup soccer venue. If you are leaving the town, there are some pleasant hotels near **San Juan del Río**. *Mexico City 132 mi/213 km.*

San Juan Del Río   D5
Querétaro (pop. 25,000). Attractive little town, renowned as a handicrafts center and home of the gem industry. Stones such as opals, aquamarine, turquoise, amethyst and topaz can be purchased here. The vineyards of San Juan are the southernmost in Mexico and some very acceptable red and white wines are produced here. Tours can be arranged to visit the cellars.

Two pleasant hotels in the area have been converted from haciendas or mansion houses — the Mansión Galindo and La Mansión. They are set in beautiful gardens with swimming pools and these relaxing surroundings offer visitors an enjoyable stay. *Mexico City 108 mi/173 km.*

San Miguel de Allende   C3
Guanajuato (pop. 36,000). The town of San Miguel de Allende is a National Monument and one of Mexico's colonial gems. It lies in a hollow against a background of hills and plains. Narrow cobblestone streets wind their way down to this charming little town of arcades and flower-filled patios. It is a thriving artistic and cultural center and has long appealed to writers and artists who have formed their own colony here. The place abounds with art galleries and boutiques selling a variety of attractive regional handicrafts. The town was founded in 1542 and gained historic importance as the birthplace of Ignacio Allende, one of the great leaders of the Independence wars against the Spanish. Originally known as San Miguel, 'Allende' was added in his honor at the end of the war. Life centers around the small main zócalo, dominated by a huge Gothic church — La Parroquia — which is the main feature of the town. The Instituto Allende was created as a center for the study of the arts and has grown into Latin America's largest school of fine arts. The San Miguel writing center specializes in writing and language. To the north of the town there is an equestrian school for horseback riding enthusiasts where they undergo intensive and professional training. About 8 miles (13 km) to the north you can visit the **Sanctuario de Atotonilco** (Sanctuary of Atotonilco) which is an important religious center. Indians from surrounding areas have made pilgrimages here for centuries. There are frescoes and sculptures depicting popular art in Mexico from the 18th century. It was the first stop for Father Hidalgo, General Allende and their troops in their battle for Independence. *Mexico City 174 mi/280 km.*

Teotihuacán   E7
México. 'Place of the Gods'. This remarkable archaeological site of great pyramids, temples and broad avenues is one of the most impressive sights in Mexico. Teotihuacán was the capital for the people known as the Teotihuacános and was probably the first real city in Central Mexico.

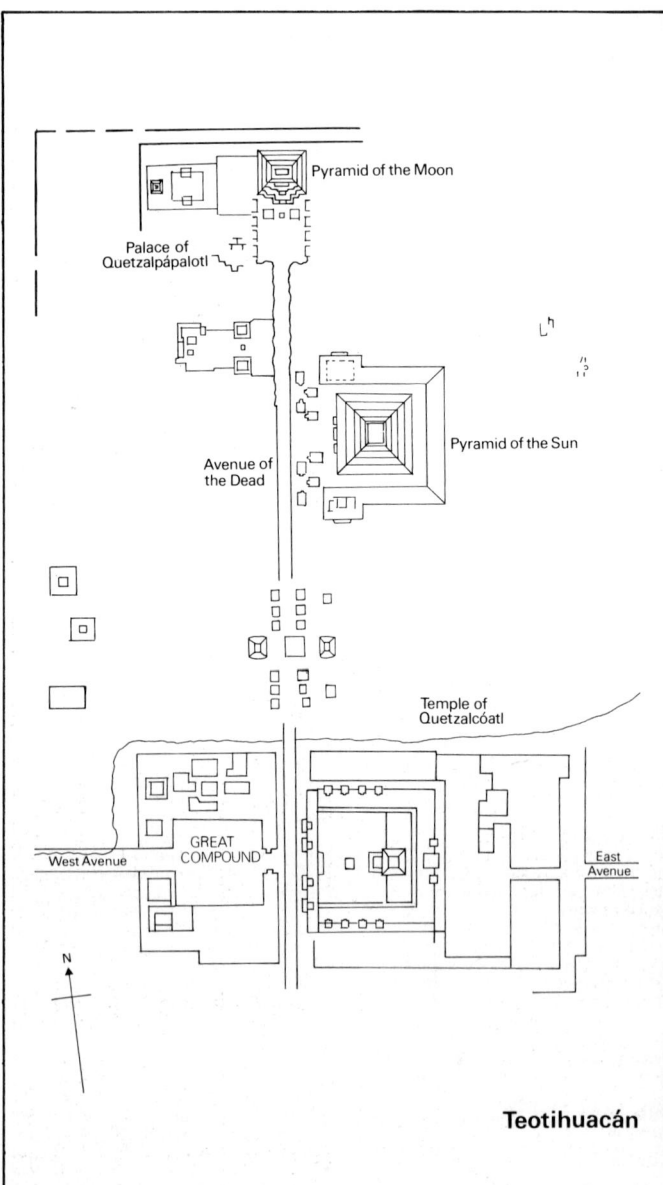

The major structures which have been discovered at Teotihuacán are believed to have been erected between about 100 BC and AD 200. During its classic period (AD 300 to 600), the city was estimated to have a population of more than 200,000. Teotihuacán influence spread over the whole area of the high plateau — it held the monopoly for the distribution of obsidian (glossy volcanic rock used in place of metal) — and conducted trade with far distant regions. Around AD 600 to 700, Teotihuacán gradually went into a decline and, for unknown reasons, the city was later abandoned.

Many experts conclude that this great capital city was taken over by barbarians from the north. The effects of Teotihuacán's decline were great and, for some time, this whole region of Central America became ungovernable with many groups of Indians making war on one another. Later, when the Aztecs arrived, they gave the deserted city the name, 'Teotihuacán', meaning 'Place where the gods were made'.

The site covers an area of more than 7 square miles (18 square kms) and is dominated by the imposing Pyramid of the Sun and Pyramid of the Moon, comparable in volume with the great pyramids of Egypt. A climb to the top gives you a magnificent view of the whole complex and the plateau on which it was built. Other particularly impressive structures are the Palace of Quetzalpápálotl (Quetzal Butterfly) and the temple of Quetzalcoatl with its carved feathered serpents, heads of deities and shell motifs — dedicated to the plumed serpent. The major buildings crown the Avenue of the Dead—a broad 2 mile (3 km) long avenue. There is a museum which houses an extensive collection of archaeological exhibits. Light and sound shows in English are staged here in the evenings at 7 pm between October and May, except for Mondays, although times and dates in Mexico do frequently change. Remember to dress warmly as it can get cold.

The 16th-century Augustinian **convent of Acolman,** which is 8 miles (13 km) away, is a fine example of Plateresque art. It has been restored and is now a museum showing how the monks lived during the colonial era. It also houses some fine paintings of the period. *Mexico City 34 mi/55 km.*

Pyramid of the Sun, Teotihuacán

Tepotzotlán   E6

México (pop. 6000). This is a pleasant little town where the main attraction is the church of Tepotzotlán facing the main square. The façade of this former Jesuit seminary is decorated with over 300 hand-carved sculptures and the interior is considered to be one of the most magnificent examples of Mexico's elaborate Churrigueresque style (see Architecture p. 11). *Mexico City 31mi/50 km.*

Tlaxcala   E8

Tlaxcala (pop. 23,000). Capital of the smallest state in Mexico. Its former inhabitants, the Tlaxcalan Indians, were bitterly opposed to the Aztecs and were never conquered by them. When Cortés marched through this region, in 1519, on his way to the Aztec capital, Tenochtitlán, the Tlaxcalans joined forces with him and fought against the Aztecs. These significant events have been traced in a mural in the Palacio de

Tlaxcala Cathedral

Gobierno (Governor's Palace) on the main square. Tlaxcala is renowned as a wool-weaving center.

Santa Ana, which is about 2 miles (3 km) away, offers fine *sarapes* (blankets). *Mexico City 72 mi/115 km.*

Toluca   F6
México (pop. 200,000). State capital and the highest major city in Mexico at 8767 ft (2670 m) above sea level. The town, which is situated in a valley, is overlooked by the majestic *Nevado de Toluca*, an extinct volcano rising to a height of 15,016 ft (4577 m).

Toluca is a busy commercial center. Its main attraction for the visitor is the famous Friday market where Indians gather from all over the region to sell their wares and the scene is one of the most colorful in Mexico.

Nevado de Toluca volcano

There is an attractive main square, flanked on one side by the Palacio de Gobierno (Governor's Palace). The Museo de Artes Populares (Museum of Popular Art) houses a fine collection of interesting folk art. The Estadio Bombonera is a World Cup soccer venue.

In the surrounding area there are a number of interesting Indian villages, each with its own specialty. About 31 miles (50 km) to the south lies **Tenancingo,** noted for its wood and palm furniture, *rebozos* (shawls) and fruit liqueurs. A few miles south of Toluca, **Metepec** produces brightly-colored pottery (the Tree of Life is its most imaginative creation). **Almoloya,** which is a short distance to the south of Metepec, is known for its hand-embroidered tablecloths and, still further south, **Tianguistengo** is famed for its *sarapes* (blankets).

The site of **Calixtlahuaca,** which is about 5 miles (8 km) northwest of Toluca, with its circular pyramid dedicated to the god of wind is well worth a visit.

The **Desierto de los Leones** (Desert of Lions), has nothing to do with lions or deserts; it is a park situated within a beautiful forest of tall pines. In the park, you can see the ruins of Santo Desierto, a 17th-century Carmelite monastery. Located between Toluca and Mexico City, **Ixtapán de la Sal** is a popular spa resort about 50 miles (80 km) to the southwest with fresh green lawns, fountains and flowers, sports facilities and natural thermal springs housed in Classical Greek and Roman style. *Mexico City 41 mi/66 km.*

Tula   D6
Hidalgo. About 53 miles (85 km) north of Mexico City lie the remains of the ancient Toltec city of Tula. The site is built on a flat plain dominated by gigantic Atlantes, columns which form part of the Temple of the Warriors. These columns, depicting warriors, are 15 ft (4.6 m) high and once supported the roof of a temple, now long gone. Tula grew in importance with the arrival of the Toltecs in the 8th century. During the early postclassic period (AD 900 to 1200) the Toltec culture dominated a vast area centered in Tula as its capital. By the middle of the 13th century the Toltecs had been driven out by Aztec invaders and Tula had been abandoned.

Between Mexico City and Tepotzotlán are two archaeological sites of some significance. In the vicinity of Tlalnepantla there is a relic of Aztec times — **Tenayuca,** a double pyramid surrounded by plumed serpents. The site of **Santa Cecilia** is nearby, set in a beautiful, tranquil garden with trees and tall cacti. Its main feature is a small pyramid surmounted by a sanctuary — the only complete example of an Aztec temple. *Mexico City 53 mi/85 km.*

Valle de Bravo   F4
México (pop. 12,000). This is a favorite weekend resort about two hours' drive west of Mexico City. It is sometimes referred to as Mexico's 'Little Switzerland' because of its chalet-style houses built amid woods surrounding a large lake. The countryside is beautiful, with waterfalls and rivers, and the climate is pleasant — warm during the day and breezes at night. This little rustic town overlooks the lake and presents a charming appearance with its whitewashed walls, stone chimneys and thatched roofs. Golf, sailing and fishing are popular pastimes here. *Mexico City 91 mi/147 km.*

The imposing head of one of the Atlantes of Tula

BAJA CALIFORNIA

Baja California (Lower California) is the long, narrow peninsula which stretches south of California on the United States border into the Pacific Ocean. It is separated from Mexico's western coastline by the Gulf of California, also known as the Sea of Cortés. 'Baja', as it is often called by its northern neighbors, consists of two states — Baja California Norte (north) and Baja California Sur (south). The peninsula runs 750 miles (1,200 km) from north to south and its width extends approximately from a minimum of 28 miles (45 km) near La Paz to a maximum of 105 miles (169 km) near the center. Baja consists largely of desert, semi-desert and mountains. Much of it is barren, with an almost lunar landscape and it is quite different in character from the rest of Mexico. There are occasional green farmlands and nearly 2000 miles (3200 km) of white sandy beaches. Its crystal clear waters, which range from deep blue to emerald are much warmer in the Gulf than on the western Pacific side. The scenery can be magnificent, with endless miles of desert and huge cacti of all shapes and sizes, below a deep blue sky. At night, the stars seem to have a special brilliance.

The northern state capital is Mexicali and La Paz is the capital of the southern state, whose boundary is marked by the 28th parallel. Baja California Sur became a state as recently as 1975 and until this period it had been somewhat isolated from the rest of the republic. Even today, southern Baja is over 4000 miles (6400 km) by road from Mexico City. Baja California Norte is much more densely populated than in the south. The summer is quite mild and dry and in the winter it can be cooler with some rain. Further south it is hot and humid in summer and milder in winter.

Two rugged mountain ranges run down the length of the peninsula, the Sierra San Pedro Mártir in the north and the Sierra de la Giganta (gigantic chain) in the south. The highest point rises to over 6000 ft (1 800 m) and much of the terrain between north and south is remote wilderness. A highway now runs from north to south but you need not stray too far from it to discover virtually unexplored, unspoiled areas.

Baja California was originally inhabited by the Cochimi Indians, now practically extinct. A number of primitive cave paintings discovered in the south are among the few relics left by Baja's earliest inhabitants. In the 16th century Cortés came here searching for gold and found pearls. Following that period, the peninsula was largely forgotten for a while.

In the 17th century the area was visited first by a Jesuit mission-builder, Father Kino from the mainland, and then by Father Salvatierra, who founded the first mission in 1697 at Loreto on the east coast. Many churches were built and Jesuit missionaries taught the Indians how to farm. They also brought with them illness and disease which spread among the Indians and greatly reduced their population. Franciscan orders, followed by Dominicans, carried on the work and many missions were built in the peninsula. The missions are long abandoned but can still be seen dotted about the area.

Loreto was the capital until it was destroyed by a storm in 1828. La Paz, which had gained importance as a pearling center, then became the new capital. At the time of the wars with the United States in the middle of the 19th century, there were movements to annex the peninsula to the States, but these were not successful. In the early 20th century some Mexican revolutionaries tried to turn it into a separate republic but were quelled by troops after the Revolution broke out in 1910.

There was some gold and silver mining towards the end of the 19th century and, during this period, the French operated a copper mine which was taken over by the Mexican Government in 1953. The island of San Marcos in the gulf of California has a saltworks and produces gypsum. Most of Baja's industry is in the north which is well irrigated and produces cotton, alfalfa, wheat, tomatoes and grapes. Pearl fishing in the south has a very long history.

Until a few years ago, the few visitors who penetrated down into the peninsula were mainly United States citizens who came to hunt and fish. In 1973 the Mexican Government inaugurated the 1050

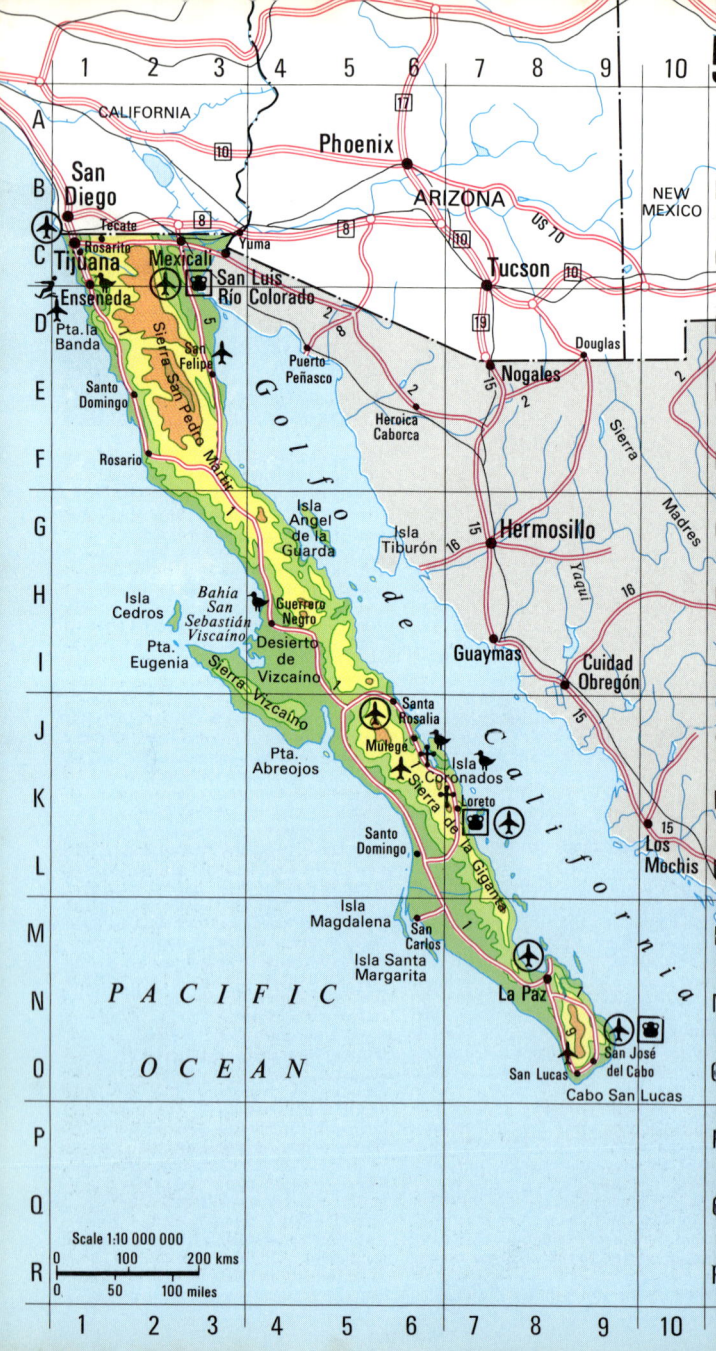

Baja California

mile (1690 km) long Transpeninsular Highway — a two-lane road connecting Tijuana in the north to Cabo San Lucas in the south. This is a well-constructed road but you are advised not to drive at night. Visitors soon began arriving and hotels were built. FONATUR, the government agency for the promotion of tourism has been developing some areas. One of the most attractive is Cabo San Lucas in the very south, where new hotels have sprung up in recent years and have in no way marred or interfered with the surroundings. The wild beauty, wide sandy beaches and magnificent rugged rock formations remain. Tourism is now a major industry in the south and main attractions are hunting, fishing, bird watching, fossil collecting and surfing. A popular interest for visitors is the unique spectacle of the mating of whales which takes place between January and March near Guerrero Negro.

Gastronomic specialities: excellent seafood from the area, abalone (fish), and turtle steak and stew; beer from Tecate near the United States border and red and white wines from Baja California Norte.

Festivals and events: Mar (2nd half) – fair, dances at Mexicali (Baja Norte); Mar 19, festival in honor of Patron Saint – San José del Cabo (Baja Sur); Apr (2nd week), transpeninsula cycle race — Ensenda, Tijuana, Mexicali (Baja Norte), La Paz (Baja Sur); May 3, anniversary of the founding of La Paz, colorful fiesta — La Paz (Baja Sur); week around May 5, International Yacht Regatta from Newport, California to Enseneda (Baja Norte); first week in June, 'Baja 500' car rally — Ensenda (Baja Norte); First Sunday in July, fiesta with processions, charros, dances — Tecate (Baja Norte); second week in Aug, 'Expo Baja California' — Tijuana (Baja Norte); Sept 4, fiesta of Santa Rosalia — Mulege (Baja Sur); Sept 8, fiesta to commemorate the Mission — Loreto (Baja Sur); Sept 16, national fiesta, *mariachis*, dances, fireworks, horseback racing — Tijuana (Baja Norte); Dec 12, fiesta of the Virgin of Guadalupe — Tecate (Baja Norte). In this ever-changing country, it is wise to check details of dates and times of events which interest you with the Mexican Tourist Office.

Cabo San Lucas O9

Baja California Sur (pop. 3000). This is now one of the major tourist areas of the Baja peninsula, located on its southernmost tip. There are a number of attractive hotels, each with its own individual character. The area is lush, with an abundance of palm trees and flowers in all shades ranging from deep pink to scarlet and violet. The big attraction is deep-sea fishing and facilities are provided. A boat ride from the harbor takes you past families of sea lions cavorting on the rocks to the famous landmark of **Baja Sur.** A spectacular series of rock formations culminates in a dramatic arch where the raging waters of the Pacific and Sea of Cortés meet and swirl through. Communications: travel by air to Mexico City via Guadalajara, to Tijuana and other Mexican cities on the west coast. Flights to several United States destinations. Ferryboat to Puerto Vallarta. *La Paz 134 mi/216 km.*

Natural arch, Cabo San Lucas

Ensenada   D1
Baja California Norte (pop. 200,000). This resort town, south of Tijuana, is popular with visitors from nearby California, USA. It is situated on the beautiful Todos Santos bay and makes a relaxing, pleasant tourist spot. The weather is pleasant in winter and not excessively hot in summer. There are plenty of shops with duty-free goods and you can visit the historic Bodegas de Santo Tomas winery. The area is a haven for fishermen; fish include the yellowtail, barracuda, bonito, albacoro and white sea bass. Boats are available on charter excursions ranging from half-day excursions to trips down the length of the peninsula and they can also be rented for whale watching. Hunting in the hinterland, surfing and riding are also popular activities. You can take a trip to Punta La Banda to see **La Bufadora** (the Snorter) — a large hollow rock through which the waves penetrate and create a blowhole. There are boat trips available which take you to see the very large elephant seals on **Guadalupe** and the **San Benito** islands. *Tijuana 67 mi/108 km.*

Pots for sale, Ensenada

Guerrero Negro   H4
Baja California Sur (pop. 5000). Guerrero Negro, which lies just inside the border of Baja California Sur state, is important for economic reasons. It is valued for its enormous salt flats, and for its oil and natural gas deposits.

Tourists, however, are more interested in 'whale watching' at nearby **Scammon Lagoon** (also known as Ojo de Liebre - the Hare's Eye) which lies about half an hour's drive away. The lagoon is located in Bahía San Sebastián Viscaíno and is about 25 miles (40 km) from Guerrero Negro. Several hundred migrating whales leave the Arctic waters in October and travel thousands of miles to take eventual refuge in the area. Between early January and mid March they calve and mate here. The area is designated as a wildlife refuge and special permission must be granted to take a boat out onto the lagoon during the mating season. The visitor can watch from the shore or, for a really good view, a small plane can be hired in Guerrero Negro to fly over the whales. *Tijuana 428 mi/688 km.*

La Paz   N
Baja California Sur (pop. 100,000). Capital of Baja California Sur. La Paz, which is a port on the eastern coast, lies in a deep inlet in the south of the state, about 50 m (80 km) north of the Tropic of Cancer. It has a history of over 400 years of pearl fishing and some of its most magnificent black and pink pearls have been used in European crown jewels. In more recent times the industry has diminished. There are good opportunities for deep-sea fishing and hunting in the vicinity. The town is not a particularly big tourist attraction in itself but it is pleasant, with laurel trees and colonial-style buildings and it is usually warm and sunny. A church, which was built in 1861, stands on a hill overlooking the main square. The harbor, or *malecón*, is pleasant to stroll along, watching the ships and there are some excellent beaches to the south. The town was first discovered, by Cortés, in 1535 and a major event in its development was the arrival of the Jesuits who built a mission here in 1720.

The town's original name, which was Bahía de la Santa Cruz (Bay of the Holy Cross), was changed to La Paz in 1596. When the Spaniard, Sebastián Vizcaíno arrived and encountered the peaceful and friendly tribe of Guaicuru Indians, he decided that the name La Paz, meaning peace, more accurately reflected the character of the people. You can travel by air to Mexico City, other Mexican cities and to Los Angeles in the United States. There is a ferryboat to Guyamas, Topolobampo, Mazatlán and Puerto Vallarta. Buses are available to travel the length of the peninsula. *Tijuana 860 mi/1384 km.*

Loreto   K
Baja California Sur (pop. 5000). Loreto is a tiny town with sandy streets, situated

he gulf coast. The first Jesuit mission was founded here in 1697 and Loreto was declared capital of the whole peninsula. In 1829 a hurricane wiped out the town, but the original mission, 'Mother Mission' in the center of town has been reconstructed and is worth visiting. The old bell tower is worth a visit. The bells, which date back to 1743, were a gift from the Spanish rulers. The museum of the Californian missions has an interesting collection of relics and historical manuscripts. Boat trips are available to **Coronados island** to see the sea lions playing on the beaches. On nearby **Isla Carmen,** thousands of tons of salt are extracted from its salt mines. FONATUR, the government agency for the promotion of tourism has a project underway for development in this area. *La Paz 221 mi/356 km.*

Mexicali C3
Baja California Norte (pop. 500,000). Mexicali is the capital of the northern state and a border town. It is the center of a rich farming area and is very Mexican in character with fine public buildings. There are no particular tourist attractions here but the Baja Museum has information on the history of the peninsula and there are bullfights almost every weekend. Hunting is particularly good in this area. *Tijuana 117 mi/189 km.*

Mulegé J6
Baja California Sur (pop. 3000). This is a delightful little oasis situated in the midst of a barren terrain at the mouth of the river Santa Rosalia. The town with its date palms, semi-tropical fruit-trees, its pleasant little square and low adobe houses is suitable for a quiet relaxing vacation. There is good river and sea fishing and boat trips are available up river or to nearby islands inhabited by sea lions. The beaches in the area are excellent. Visitors can cross the river to see the **Misión de Santa Rosalia** which was founded by the Jesuits in 1705. Modest accommodations. *La Paz 308 mi/495 km.*

Rosarito H4
Baja California Norte This beach resort south of Tijuana was very popular in the 1920s and 1930s with Hollywood film stars. Now it is a particularly favorite resort for families from the northern border towns. There are excellent beaches and opportunities for horseback riding. *Tijuana 16 mi/26 km.*

San Felipe E3
Baja California Norte (pop. 15,000). A little fishing village on the east coast which is growing as a tourist center. There are sandy beaches, warm waters and good fishing. *Mexicali 125 mi/200 km.*

San José del Cabo O9
Baja California Sur (pop. 12,000). Small town situated right on the south coast of the peninsula near Cabo San Lucas. This semitropical town is an important commercial and agricultural center. There is a pleasant little main square overlooked by an old church and the House of Culture has an interesting museum and library. The beaches in the vicinity are very good. Airport Los Cabos serves both San José and Cabo San Lucas. You can travel by air to Mexico City via Guadalajara, Tijuana and other Mexican cities on the west coast. There are flights to several United States destinations. *La Paz 115 mi/185 km.*

Santa Rosalía J6
Baja California Sur(pop. 10,000). In itself Santa Rosalía is not a great attraction but there are some beautiful beaches nearby. The town, which is on the east coast of the peninsula, was founded in 1855 by a rancher who discovered rich copper deposits here. *Tijuana 562 mi/904 km.*

Tecate C1
Baja California Norte (pop. 10,000). This border town between Tijuana and Mexicali is most famous for its excellent Tecate beer. Tecate is very Mexican in character. On the outskirts of the town there is a community crafts center where there are fine handicrafts for sale. *Tijuana 30 mi/49 km.*

Tijuana C1
Baja California Norte (pop. 1,000,000). Famous (or infamous) border town, situated at the most westerly point of Mexico. This prosperous town, which is the sixth largest in Mexico, has the reputation of being brash, vulgar and fun. Although it used to be viewed as seedy and tawdry, it has since been cleaned up. Tijuana is popular with visitors from the United States (especially those from nearby California) who come in their millions for short visits. Many venture no further into Mexico. The town offers gambling and many sports such as dog racing, *jai alai*(or *frontón*) and bullfighting. The drive from San Diego takes about half an hour and the visitor enters another world which is very Latin and full of noise and color. Shopping is also a big attraction as it is a duty-free zone and shops are crammed with goods of every description. Alcohol is cheap and the original village became very popular with thirsty Californians who came here during prohibition. Restaurants are lively in the evening. *Mexico City 1830 mi/2945 km.*

Glass worker, Tijuana

THE NORTHWEST

The two large states, Sonora and Sinaloa and the small state of Nayarit make up this area. The northwest is one of the most productive regions in Mexico. Although it is mostly semi-desert, the flat lands between the Sierra Madre Occidental range and the coast contain several rivers. In the early part of this century, during the presidential terms of Obregón and Calles who were both from this region, a system of dams was constructed which enabled the desert to flourish. This important agricultural area now produces wheat, safflower, soyabeans, cotton, alfalfa and tomatoes. Cattle is raised to provide a large beef market.

Sonora state is a contrasting mixture of high mountains and vast expanses of arid desert. The terrain becomes sub-tropical further south in the state of Sinaloa and tropical in Nayarit. There are miles of beautiful coastline, plush resorts, good fishing and hunting. Guaymas, in Sonora, and Mazatlán, which is further south in Sinaloa, are favorite resorts. The summer months are extremely hot in the northern states. In the winter, the climate remains quite pleasant, although there can be extremes of cold and even snow in December or January in the northerly mountains. The jungles of Nayarit are hot and humid throughout the year.

The northwest is the home of Yaqui Indians, but there are few relics of their ancestors or traces of past civilizations in this part of Mexico. Sonora and its neighboring states Sinaloa, Durango and Chihuahua became part of the province of Nueva Viscaya under Spanish rule in the 16th century. Over a century later Fray Eusébio Francisco Kino led a missionary expedition to the area and founded a number of towns. During the Civil War in the United States, Sonora was coveted by its northern neighbor but Don Porfirio Díaz saw the potential of this area for Mexico and started to develop it. Ironically, when the Revolution broke out in 1910, some of the most powerful figures who brought about his downfall were from Sonora. They proceeded to rule the country for about a quarter of a century and are referred to as the 'Sonora dynasty'. The Revolution brought prosperity to the area as modern farming techniques were introduced. Sonora now produces enough wheat to feed the country and the rest is exported.

Mazatlán, as a big deep-sea fishing center and port, has attracted many tourists to this area. Remote Nayarit is the home of

the Huichol and Cora Indians who are among the most interesting of groups in Mexico. The Huichols go on expeditions into remote areas to collect the peyote bean which is supposed to be possessed of magical powers and, under its influence, they produce strange and mystical pictures.

Gastronomic specialties: Sonora is famed for its beef which is probably the best in Mexico. The specialty is dried beef, known as *machace*. A special delicacy from Sinaloa and Sonora is a solid shrimp soup known as *caldo sudador*. Guayamas is famed for its shrimps and the seafood in Mazatlán is excellent.

Festivals and events: Jan 30, fiesta, San Blas (Nayarit); Feb or Mar (begins week before Lent), very colorful Mazatlán carnival (Sinaloa); Jun 1, fishing festival, Guaymas (Sonora); Jun 29, feast of St Peter and St Paul, Mexcaltitlán (Nayarit); Jul and Sep, International fishing tournaments, Guaymas (Sonora); Sep 15, opening of fishing season — procession led by bishop to bless the fleet, Mazatlán (Sinaloa); end Oct or beginning Nov, International fishing tournament, Mazatlán (Sinaloa). In this ever-changing country, it is wise to check details of dates and times of events which interest you with the Mexican Tourist Office.

Álamos   H9

Sonora (pop. 6000). Álamos is a charming colonial city which has been preserved as a National Monument. It is one of the earliest Spanish settlements and was once the capital of Sonora. Its main square, Plaza de Armas, is surrounded by arcades and fine buildings, overlooked by the 18th-century Church of La Señora de la Concepción. Hunting and fishing enthusiasts will find this area to be worth spending some of their time in. The famous Mexican jumping bean grows in the surrounding hills. The bean is activated by a hyperactive larva. *Guadalajara 679 mi/1093 km.*

Culiacán K11

Sinaloa (pop. 324,000). Capital of the state. The name is derived from the Nahuatl word 'Colhuacan' which means 'place where the god Coltzin is revered' The town was built on an old Indian settlement and is now a mining and agricultural center. The architecture is partly colonial and partly modern with a fine cathedral on the zócalo and some recent, striking architecture. Fishing is good at **Adolfo López Mateos** reservoir which is a short distance to the northeast and at the nearby lakes of **Bataoto, San Lorenzo, Cascabeles** and **Mariquita.** There are thermal springs at **Imala, Macurimi, Carrizalejo, Vigía** and **Arenitas.** *Guadalajara 454 mi/731 km.*

Guaymas G7

Sonora (pop. 100,000). Guaymas, which is not far from Hermosillo, is one of Mexico's major seaports. The setting is dramatic as the mountains and desert sweep down to the sea. The town was founded in 1771 and became a general trading port in 1841 as an outlet for the rich minerals from Sonora. From 1847-48 it was occupied by United States naval forces and was then almost seized in battle by a French pirate and his gang in 1854. The French, under Maximilian, did succeed in taking over the port in 1865.

Guaymas can be viewed as two parts. The older section is characterized by its 18th-century church of San Francisco, its shrimp docks and freighters. The new section which is across the other side of a mountainous peninsula, consists of a resort area with bays and luxurious hotels. Guaymas is renowned for its variety of seashells, and its fishing opportunities are among the best in the world. The area is good for hunting and there are facilities for riding. To the south of the town there is a reservation of Yaqui Indians, a fierce tribe who fought bravely for the preservation of their lands. There is a ferry boat available from Guaymas to Santa Rosalía in Baja California Sur. *Guadalajara 800 mi/1287 km.*

Hermosillo F7

Sonora (pop. 400,000). State capital and seat of the state university. The town was settled in 1742 and later named after one of Mexico's leaders in the Wars of Independence, José María González Hermosillo. Local architecture is a combination of colonial and modern. The shops here are worth visiting. Several prominent Mexican presidents came from Sonora

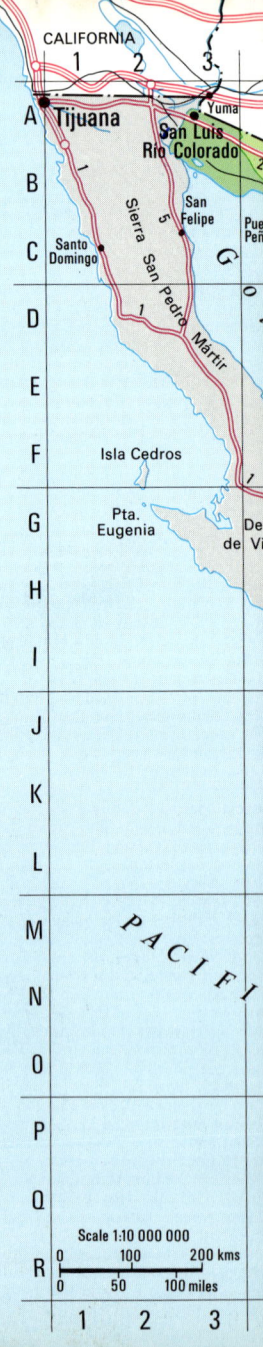

and are honored by monuments — Adolfo de la Huerta, Alvaro Obregón, Plutarco Elías Calles. Places of interest are the Central Plaza Zaragoza, the cathedral and to the southeast, and Madero Park which is a popular promenade and sports center. The Rodríguez Dam (named after Aberlardo Rodríguez who promoted industry in the area) holds the waters of the Río Sonora and has played a significant role in converting this desert area into an important agricultural producer. *Guadalajara 884 mi/1423 km.*

Kino Bay   F6
Sonora. About 70 miles west of Hermosillo, you can find Kino Bay. New Kino has magnificent beaches and there are plans for major tourist development here including a marina, hotels etc. The fishing is excellent. There are a number of offshore islands, the largest of which is **Tiburón** (shark island) which is being developed as an important wildlife and game refuge. Not far from Kino Bay there is a camp of Seri Indians — remaining survivors of the tribe which inhabited the area when Father Kino came over from the mainland to bring them Christianity. You may find them producing their rather fine ironwood animal carvings. *Guadalajara 951 mi/1530 km.*

Los Mochis   J9
Sinaloa (pop. 135,000). Los Mochis means 'little turtles'. Since irrigation was introduced to the region Los Mochis has become an important producer of rice, cotton, sugar cane, winter vegetables and marigolds, of which the city has a profusion. Los Mochis itself has few attractions for the tourist but it is the major Pacific terminal for the Chihuahua Pacific railroad which reaches the end of the line at Topolobampo about 15 miles (21 km) away. This is considered one of the most scenic railway journeys in the world as it passes through **Barranca del Cobre** (Copper Canyon) between here and Chihuahua (see Chihuahua and section on internal travel — rail) *Guadalajara 582 mi/937 km.*

Mazatlán   M12
Sinaloa (pop. 186,000). Mazatlán, in Nahuatl, means 'the place of the deer'. It lies just a short distance south of the Tropic of Cancer on the Pacific coast. The setting in which the town lies is lovely and the beaches are superb. Mazatlán is often

Sunset viewed from Mazatlán

referred to as the 'Pearl of the Pacific'. It is Mexico's largest Pacific port and ferryboats leave here every evening for La Paz in Baja California Sur which lies 235 miles (378 km) across the Gulf of California.

The Chibchas Indians originally inhabited Mazatlán but when the Spaniards arrived, the town began to prosper as the port was used to ship gold and silver to Spain. It soon became prey to attacks from invading pirates. A permanent Spanish colony began to take root in the early 1800s and by the end of the 19th century Mazatlán had grown into an important port and center of a large fishing industry, world famous for marlin and sailfish. Some of its beaches have huge rollers which attract surfing enthusiasts and there is also sailing, scuba diving, water skiing, golf and tennis. The town is lively

Beach at Mazatlán

and restaurants are swinging. An enjoyable way of seeing the town is to travel by *pulmonia* — a sort of three-wheeled taxi resembling a motor scooter which puffs its way up the steep streets. A stroll along the palm-lined sea front is very pleasant, especially at sunset when huge rollers are crashing onto the shore. Local boys perform a miniature version of the performance by the cliff divers of Acapulco when they dive into the sea from the jutting out rock, El Mirador.

There are magnificent views of the city from the Spanish fort overlooking the old harbor, and from Cerro de la Nevería (Icebox Hill).

Mazatlán is a very popular destination for fishermen and hunters, with plenty of facilities for expeditions. In the hinterland there are many varieties of game: deer, jaguar, mountain lion, coyote, wild boar and ocelot. The aquarium center has over 200 varieties of fish and is well worth a visit.

There are bullfights in the winter season. Two events, in particular, are big attractions in Mazatlán: the Mazatlán Carnival which is a sort of Mardi Gras, takes place from the Friday until the Tuesday before Lent with music and dancing, fireworks, floats and much color and fun. On September 15th, just before the Independence Day celebrations, the bishop of Mazatlán leads a procession down to the harbor to bless the fleet and open the fishing season.

Mazatlán is a gateway for traveling across to Baja California by ship and is a port of call for cruise ships which journey down the Pacific coast from the United States. *Guadalajara 314 mi/505 km.*

Mexcaltitlán N13

Nayarit (pop. 2000). Mexcaltitlán is a Nahuatl word meaning 'the house on the moon'. This unique little island village with its streets which radiate outwards, is built on a lagoon near the mouth of the San Pedro river. The setting bears similarities to the Aztec capital of Tenochtitlán which was also built on a lake and there is speculation as to whether Mexcaltitlán was the original center of the Aztec tribe. An unusual festival is held on June 29th — the feast of St. Peter and St. Paul when there is a race around the island by a pair of canoes manned by images of the saints. *Guadalajara 208 mi/335 km.*

Nogales C7

Sonora (pop. 75,000). Largest border town in Sonora and a busy port of entry for tourists from neighboring towns of Tucson and Phoenix in the United States. Important center for ranching, dairying and irrigated farming. *Guadalajara 1056 mi/1700 km.*

San Blas O14

Nayarit (pop. 5000). Tropical seaside village with unpaved streets and adobe huts — a place for escapists. It appealed to the poet Longfellow who wrote his last poem here, the *Bells of San Blas*, during his exploration of the northwest Pacific. Beyond the village is **Old San Blas** with the ruins of a fortress and an old mission built by the Spaniards. The area is excellent for deep-sea fishing. You can take a 2½ hour jungle boat trip along the river San Cristóbal to **La Tobara springs,** passing along green tunnels of exotic vegetation and crystal-clear waters. *Guadalajara 185 mi/297 km.*

Tepic O14

Nayarit (pop. 150,000). State capital situated at the foot of the extinct volcano Sangangüey. The town is an interesting combination of old and new. It was an old Indian site occupied by Spaniards in 1542 but remained isolated and developed little until the early part of this century when the railroad arrived in the area.

Eighteenth century buildings of note are the cathedral with its fine Gothic towers and the church of the Holy Cross which was once part of a Franciscan convent. The regional museum houses pre-Columbian ceramics. Shops stock colorful items produced by the Huichol and Cora Indians who live in the surrounding hills, in much the same way as they have for centuries. A journey north of Tepic towards Bellavista brings you to Indian country.

Excursions can be made to **El Salto** – a magnificent waterfall west of the city, and to the **Laguna Santa Maria** – a volcanic crater lake lying about 20 mi (32 km) to the southeast. A drive south of Tepic, in the direction of Puerto Vallarta, takes you through the 'lunar landscape' of the **Ceboruco lava fields.** *Guadalajara 141 mi/227 km.*

Topolobampo J9

Sinaloa (pop. 5000). The name has been interpreted as 'tiger water' or 'lion's watering place'. This is the end of the journey for the scenic Chihuahua Railroad trip from Chihuahua which then returns to Chihuahua from here. Ferries depart from Topolobambo Sur to La Paz in Baja California. The off-shore island of **El Farallón** is a refuge for sea lions and there are wildlife sanctuaries for large varieties of birds on other nearby islands. There are plenty of good beaches in the area and shell hunting and beachcombing are popular pastimes. *Guadalajara 597 mi/961 km*

THE NORTH

Within this vast area which comprises the five states of Aguascalientes, Chihuahua, Coahuila, Durango and Zacatecas, there are extreme differences of history, culture and terrain. It includes the largest and one of the most important states in Mexico, namely Chihuahua which borders on New Mexico and Texas in the United States. Chihuahua has some of the most dramatic scenery in Mexico. The Barranca del Cobre (Copper Canyon), with endless miles of mountains, canyons and deep gorges, combines with extensive areas of desert, plains and cultivated land. It also abounds in rivers, forests, caves and waterfalls — the waters of the Basaseáchic Falls drop 1000 ft (305 m) and this cascade is one of the most spectacular in Mexico. The North has much to offer, with its wealth of industry and good hunting. One of its major attractions for the visitor is the Chihuahua Pacific railroad, which journeys through the Copper Canyon from the border town of Ojinaga south to Los Mochis on the west coast. Chihuahua town is a convenient place to begin your train journey. The train passes through countless tunnels and over many bridges crossing the high Sierras with the most incredible panoramas at every turn. This is the home of the Tarahumara Indians, who live in very primitive conditions and whose civilization is gradually dwindling. The wild and rugged country of the State of Durango has been the scene for many western films.

In the early 1800s Texas was claimed by the state of Coahuila (which means 'place of leafy trees'). Many important battles took place in this area during the Independence Wars and a number of the leaders of the Revolution came from the region. Cattle ranching and steel and silver mining are the main industries. The region has many historic sites, pleasant colonial towns and industrialized modern cities.

Gastronomic specialties: excellent beef, cheese and apples from Chihuahua; cheese soup which resembles Swiss fondue and is normally eaten with tortillas.

Festivals and events: Apr 20-May 1, San Marcos Fair, Aguascalientes (Aguascalientes); May 19-22, fiesta de Santa Rita, Chihuahua (Chihuahua); Jul 8, commemoration of founding of city of Durango (Durango); Aug 6, Festival of Cristo de la Capilla, Saltillo (Coahuila); Aug 10, fiesta of San Lorenzo (Chihuahua); Aug 13-21, traditional fair, Saltillo (Coahuila); Oct 4, festival and wine fair, Sal-

tillo (Coahuila); Dec 4, fiesta of Santa Bárbara, Ciudad Juárez (Chihuahua). In this ever-changing country, it is wise to check details of dates and times of events with the Mexican Tourist Office.

Aguascalientes N8

Aguascalientes (pop. 300,000). State capital, named for its hot thermal springs. This is an attractive city with a very pleasant climate. There are several interesting churches near the main zócalo such as the Cathedral in which there is a famous painting by José Alzibar, the *Adoration of the Kings*. The neo-Byzantine San Antonio church is worth visiting and the temple of our Lord of Encino with its Black Christ is also of interest.

The area is an important producer of wine and visits can be arranged to local wineries. The region is renowned for the breeding of fighting bulls. Aguascalientes is famous for its prettily embroidered clothes and you can make some good buys here. From April 20 to the end of the month you can attend the famous annual San Marcos Fair which has bullfights, rodeos and fireworks.

The hot springs of San Nicolás de la Cantera, Ojo Caliente and Colombo are nearby. *Guadalajara 156 mi/251 km.*

Chihuahua F4

Chihuahua (pop. 480,000). Capital of the largest state in Mexico. Chihuahua lies on a high plateau with the Sierra Madre mountain range to the west. This prosperous city is an important commercial center for ranching and timber. It is most famous as the breeding ground for the tiny Chihuahua dogs, although they are somewhat scarce and quite expensive.

Chihuahua was founded in 1709 and named San Francisco de Cuellar. In 1718 it was declared a town and renamed San Felip de Real de Chihuahua — later short-

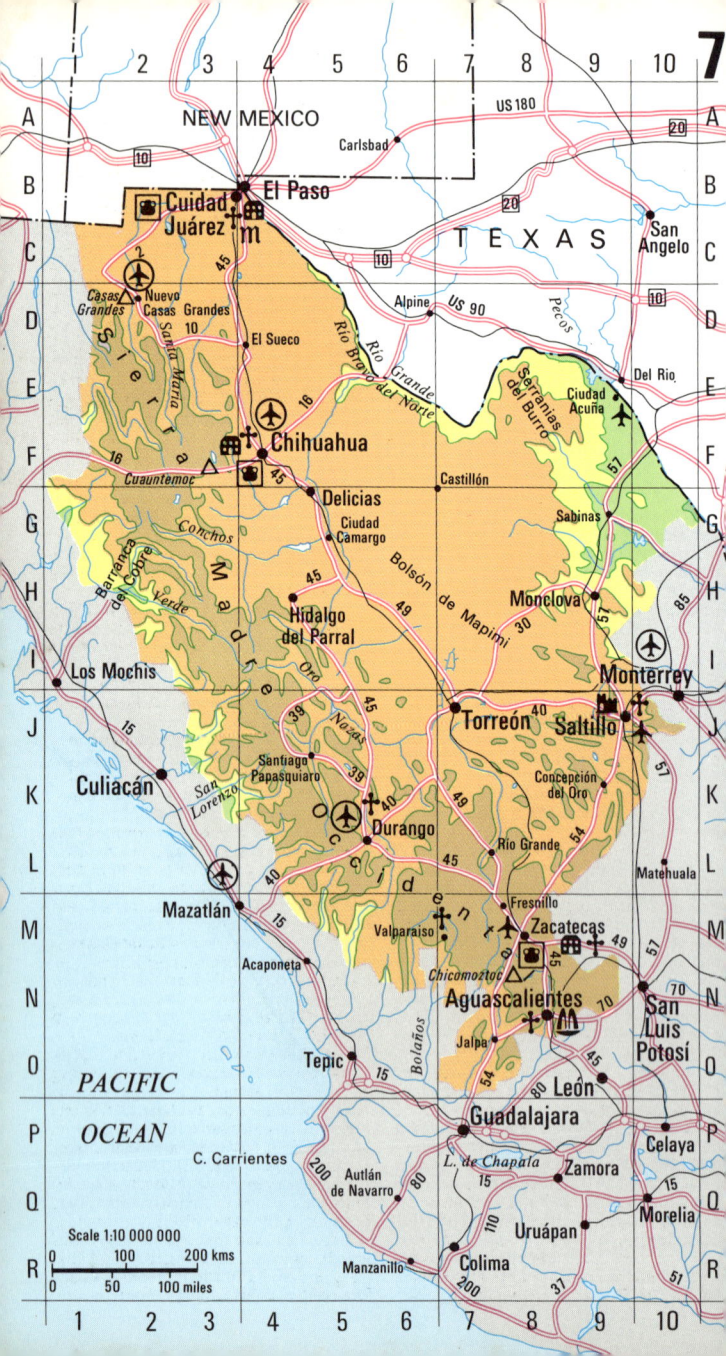

View of the Copper Canyon

ened to Chihuahua following Independence from the Spaniards. The town began to prosper when silver discoveries were made in the late 17th century and it has played an important role in history. The leader of the struggle for Independence, Padre Miguel Hidalgo, was captured here by the Spanish forces and executed in 1811. Notorious revolutionary Pancho Villa, who played a significant role in the Revolution of 1910-1920, which overthrew the 30 year regime of President Porfirio Díaz, made his home here.

The city has wide avenues, elegant squares and interesting buildings such as the large Baroque 18th-century cathedral; the Palacio Federal (Federal Palace) where Father Hidalgo and his followers were imprisoned by the Spaniards in 1811; Palacio de Gobierno (State capital) where they were subsequently executed. The Church of San Francisco, which was built in 1721, is the oldest church in Chihuahua. The Quinta Luz museum has great historical interest. This was formerly the home of Pancho Villa and was used as his headquarters during the height of the Revolution. The museum houses such items as firearms and the bullet-riddled car in which Villa was ambushed and killed.

Chihuahua is surrounded by some spectacular lush green scenery. The **Cascada de Basaseáchic** (Basaseáchic Falls) is a waterfall with a drop of more than 1000 ft (305 m) which spills down into the beautiful jade-green pools in the canyon below. The falls can be reached by driving past the towns of Cuauhtémoc and La Junta and then taking a mountain road to Ocampo, the site of the falls. The **Sierra de Tarahumara,** home of the Tarahumara Indians, is an area of breathtaking beauty, with vast mountain ranges, gorges and canyons. The **Barranca del Cobre** (Copper Canyon) rivals the Grand Canyon in Arizona for size. The **Chihuahua Pacific railway** passes through here traveling south through vast canyons, some up to 4000 ft (1219 m) deep and a mile (1½ km) across. A good place to board is Chihuahua (the journey begins in the border town of Ojinaga) and travel down to Los Mochis or Topolobampo on the west coast. (See p. 16.) This route has been called 'the world's most scenic railroad' and is a big attraction.

There is also quite a large Mennonite population in the area. They settled here in the 1920s and are a hardworking people, producing such goods as pears, apples and cheese.

There are some impressive ruins at **Casas Grandes,** about 4 miles (6 km) from the town of Nuevo Casas Grandes. These ruins were once a great city and there are traces of the Pueblo Indians and the Mesoamerican cultures. There are some attractive lodges to accommodate hunters who will find hunting opportunities to be good. *Mexico City 895 mi/1440 km.*

Ciudad Juárez   C3

Chihuahua (pop. 700,000). Ciudad Juárez is one of Mexico's most important border cities and its character is an interesting combination of Mexican and Texan. The town was originally called Paso del Norte but it was renamed Ciudad Juárez in honor of Benito Juárez in 1888 — one of Mexico's most popular presidents.

Ciudad Juárez is very much a border town. There are pleasant, tree-lined boulevards and impressive statues of Juárez and Abraham Lincoln. Buildings of note include the headquarters of the Juárez government and the Mission of our Lady of Guadalupe, built in 1659 to commemorate the Patron saint of Mexico. The museum of Art and History in the new Juárez cultural center is worth visiting for its pre-Columbian artifacts and handicrafts. There are two bull rings and the nightlife is lively. *Chihuahua 233 mi/375 km.*

Durango L6

Durango (pop. 250,000). State capital. Durango was founded in 1563 and named after the city Durango in Spain. A short time later, gold and silver deposits were found in the area and, as a result, Durango grew in prosperity. Cerro del Mercado (Market Hill), to the north, is one of the largest iron deposits in the world. Durango has become famous as the setting for numerous Hollywood Westerns. Many of the film sets are still standing and can be visited, sometimes even if they are in use, provided that prior permission has been granted. The huge Tuscan-style 18th-century cathedral, facing the main square, is said to be haunted.

The surrounding landscape is wild and rugged. Nearby, you can visit the thermal springs of Navacoyán and Valparaiso, whose waters are rich in sulphur, iron and many healing minerals. *Guadalajara 372 mi/598 km.*

Monclova H9

Coahuila (pop. 150,000). This attractive old town is worth a stop. It was once the capital of Texas while Texas was part of Mexican territory. Monclova is now an important steel city where the gigantic steel mill, Altos Hornos, produces about one third of Mexico's steel output. *Mexico City 671 mi/1080 km.*

Saltillo J9

Coahuila (pop. 300,000). State capital. Saltillo is a pleasant city with a mild dry climate. It was founded in 1575 by Captain Alberto del Canto who used the area as a teaching center for primitive Indians in the north of Mexico. The city developed into an important center. There are vineyards, lovely walnut trees and some fine Baroque churches. The cathedral of Santiago on the Plaza de Armas square was built from 1746-1801 and is a magnificent example of Churrigueresque architecture (for an explanation of this term, see p. 11). The Fortress of Carlota which is in the old part of town near the Plaza de Armas was dedicated to Emperor Maxmilian's wife.

Saltillo is famous for its colorful *sarapes*, its textile industry, pottery and silverware.

You can take a fascinating rail trip through narrow mountain ridges to the old silver mining town of **Concepción de Oro**. The old railway coaches, which are still used today, were built in 1895 and are heated by wood burning stoves. *Mexico City 543 mi/873 km.*

Torreón J7

Coahuila (pop. 290,000). Torreón is an important industrial and cattle growing center and produces cotton, wheat, dairy products and machinery. It was founded in 1875 on the site of an old ranch. This is wine country and visits can be arranged to vineyards and distilleries. *Mexico City 615 mi/989 km.*

Zacatecas M8

Zacatecas (pop. 80,000). State capital. The name is derived from the Nahuatl word, meaning 'place of hay or grass', and was originally inhabited by the Zacateco Indians. Zacatecas is built on the mountain known as Cerro de la Bufa and is surrounded by a ring of tall mountain ranges. The town is picturesque and carefully conserved, with steep cobblestone streets. It was founded in 1546 by the Spanish and silver mines discovered in the area soon led to prosperity. A vast quantity of silver was produced from this region between the 16th and 19th centuries.

There are some fine examples of colonial architecture such as the cathedral on the south side of the main square. It was completed in 1752 as a product of the wealth of this mining town. The Baroque church of Santo Domingo, to the west of the plaza, is worth visiting and the Palacio de Gobierno (Governor's Palace) and Teatro de Calderón (Theater of Calderon) are also fine examples of Spanish colonial architecture. The chapel of La Capilla de los Remedios, built on the summit of La Bufa mountain, affords you an excellent view of the city. Inside the chapel, there is an image of the Virgin, believed by the local Indians to have magical powers. The convent of Nuestra Señora de Guadalupe, to the south of town, is considered one of Mexico's most important buildings. It has been converted to a museum housing valuable paintings from colonial times and a collection of rare books.

You can make an interesting journey traveling by miniature train to the abandoned El Eden mine. The **ruins of Chicomoztoc**, referred to as Las Ruinas Quemadas (the burnt ruins) are about 30 mi (48 km) southwest of Zacatecas. They have remained fairly well preserved as a result of the dry climate here. The ruins cover quite an extensive area which is divided into three sections — the temple, the citadel and the palace. Evidence suggests the roots of this culture could have been in Teotihuacán from AD 300 — 500. *Mexico City 381 mi/613 km.*

THE NORTHEAST

This region comprises the two states, Nuevo León and San Luis Potosí. Its terrain is a combination of cultivated farmlands and arid plains, where the flat lands of the border area rise up into the Sierra Madre Oriental range. The southern area extends into the tropical jungles of the Gulf of Mexico. Although the area is not a common tourist destination, many visitors pass through from Nuevo Laredo on the United States border on their way to Mexico City. There are numerous places to visit and some of the scenery is magnificent. Parts of the journey take you over winding roads with magnificent views of the high peaks, canyons and valleys of the Sierra Madres. The region is sparsely populated. The climate is extremely hot and dry in the summer and very cold at the height of winter, especially at high altitudes, where it can snow heavily.

The conquest of the north was very difficult for the Spaniards and they encountered fierce resistance from the nomadic tribes who wandered about the land. Indians managed to keep the major cities isolated from the rest of colonial Mexico until the middle of the 17th century when a route was finally opened, linking Monterrey to the Gulf port of Tampico. Today Monterrey, as the third largest city in Mexico, is a dynamic industrial center and acts as a crossroads for the north of Mexico, linking it to the United States and the rest of Mexico. The state of Nuevo León is very important to Mexico's economic well-being.

Chemical, steel, cement, glass, fibre, lead, silver and zinc industries are thriving and Mexican beer is also produced in the region by one of the country's largest distilleries.

Facilities for hunting are good and there are many ranches. Bullfights and charreadas are popular sports in Monterrey particularly.

Gastronomic specialties: Monterrey offers a tasty dish of *cabrito* (baby goat) which is usually grilled. Broiled ribs of beef are a specialty of Neuvo León state and in the area of San Luis Potosí, delicious dishes of tripe are served in a thick soup. The area is also renowned for its *quesadillas* — leftovers made of cheese and stuffed corn dough.

Festivals and events: Jan 20, festival of San Sebastián, San Luis Potosí (San Luis Potosí); May 20, agricultural trade fair of one month with fireworks, bullfights and horse racing, Monterrey (Nuevo León). Aug 25, festival of St Louis

the King (Dia de San Luis Rey) — celebrations in honor of San Luis Potosí's patron saint with processions and dancing (San Luis Potosí). In this ever-changing country, it is wise to check details of dates and times of events with the Mexican Tourist Office.

Monterrey   C5
Nuevo León (pop. 1,500,000). State capital. Monterrey is built in a valley surrounded by the high mountain peaks of the Sierra Madre range. It is the third largest city in Mexico and is a major industrial center with thriving steel, cement, glassware and beer industries. Monterrey was established by the Spanish captain, Diego de Monteymayor. The town was called Monterey after the Spanish Viceroy, the Count of Monterey. The second 'r' was later added to the name to avoid confusion with Monterey in the United States.

Monterrey was the scene of fighting during the wars between Mexico and the United States in the mid-1800s and during the Mexican Revolution of 1910-20. The cathedral, which overlooks the main square, has a fine tower, carved façade, sculptures and murals. El Obispado (Bishop's Palace), which was built in 1782, has been well restored. It is situated on a hill and affords a lovely panoramic view of the city. The museum within is also very interesting. The Palacio de Gobierno (Government Palace) is a good example of colonial-style architecture. The planetarium in the Alfa Cultural Center is worth a visit. Visits can also be arranged to the Cuauhtémoc Brewery which is the largest in Mexico and produces Carta Blanca and Bohemia beer.

There are some beautiful spots in the vicinity such as the **Huasteca canyon** to the southwest — a 1000 ft (300 m) gorge with huge dramatic rock formations. The **García caves,** which lie about 28 miles

The Northeast

Charreadas are popular in Monterrey

The Northeast

Monterrey

(45 km) to the northwest, are among the largest and most spectacular in the country, with great chambers, grottos and a subterranean lake. The **Chipinique Mesa,** which lies about 12 miles (19 km) to the southwest, is a very scenic spot located among the pine-clad slopes of the Sierra Madres and from here you have a wonderful view of the lush valleys spread out below. This is a popular resort area where people have summer homes and there is a restaurant.

One of the biggest attractions is the magnificent **Cola de Caballo** (Horsetail Falls) which are about 26 miles (42 km) southwest of the city. Beside the main waterfall there is a triple cascade called the **Three Graces.** Facilities include a restaurant and swimming pool. From here you can walk or travel by horse or donkey (available on hire) to the waterfall. *Mexico City 599 mi/963 km.*

San Luis Potosí   H4

San Luis Potosí(pop. 350,000). State capital. San Luis Potosí is an attractive mining town with pleasant colonial buildings, narrow streets and parks. It was inhabited by the Chicunec Indians for about 300 years before the arrival of the Spanish and was known as Tangamaga. Gold and silver deposits attracted the Spanish to the area which became a very important mining center. The town was founded by Fray Magdalena and Captain Caldera in 1592 and named San Luis Potosí after Louis, monarch of France. Potosí, which in Indian means 'extremely wealthy', was named after the rich Bolivian mines called 'potosí'.

Among the town's most notable buildings are the cathedral on the main square, begun in 1670, which exhibits styles of Baroque, Byzantine, Doric and Gothic architecture; east of the square, with its domes of many colors, there lies the church of our Lady of Carmen; the Palacio de Gobierno (Governor's Palace), is of some historical interest as it was here that leader Benito Juárez denied clemency to the overthrown Emperor Maximilian and Gonzalez Bocanegra wrote the Mexican national anthem here in 1854.

In San Luis, you can buy *rebozos* — colorful shawls which are produced in the little village of **Santa María del Río** which is 29 miles (47 km) to the south. This is ranch country and there are many large ranches in the area. *Mexico City 259 mi/417 km.*

Chihuahua Cathedral (see p. 111)

THE GULF REGION

The three states of Tamaulipas, Veracruz and Tabasco which border the Gulf of Mexico make up this region. This narrow stretch of land follows the eastward curve of Mexico and contains within it contrasting climatic conditions. The north is hot and arid. In the central state of Veracruz there are temperate and subtropical areas, dominated by the snow-capped Pico de Orizaba which rises to an altitude of over 18,000 ft (5500 m) — the highest peak in the land. Tabasco, to the south, is a region of hot and steamy rain forests.

The northern state of Tamaulipas borders the United States and towns, Nuevo Laredo and Matamoros are major border crossing points into Mexico. This area consists mainly of desert and irrigated farmlands, gradually becoming subtropical as you travel south past the Tropic of Cancer to the hot, tropical land of the south. The route passes through lush orchid jungles and fruit orchards of oranges and tangerines. Veracruz state, which is rich in agriculture, abounds in tobacco and coffee plantations. Some of the scenery is magnificent with fresh green tropical vegetation, an abundance of brilliantly colored flowers and beautiful lagoons, crowned by the snow-covered mountain peak.

There are regions of great cultural and historical interest. The Olmecs are believed to have established the earliest civilization in Mexico, settling in southern Veracruz and northern Tabasco before 1000 BC. They constructed large temples, ceremonial centers, sculptures and giant heads. A number of the huge sculptures discovered in the region were brought to the town of Villahermosa in Tabasco and are displayed in the outdoor garden La Venta museum. Their culture spread from the Valley of Mexico to Central America and influenced other civilizations which followed, including the Teotihuacános and the Maya. At the sacred city of the Totanac civilization, called El Tajín, you can visit the seven-storey Pyramid of the Niches which was built, probably with 365 niches decorating the whole building. The Huasteca Indians were a primitive people who inhabited the region to the south of Tampico. Their descendants live in the area and the majority still converse in their native tongue, speaking little or no Spanish.

Cortés landed in Veracruz in 1519 to begin the long march to the Aztec city of Tenochtitlán and the eventual conquest of Mexico. The subsequent destruction of the Aztec civilization changed the whole course of Mexico's history and caused the merger of two important cultures — that of the ancient Indian civilizations and the Hispanic culture. During the Mexican/United States War, following Independence, United States forces landed at Veracruz in 1847 and marched to Mexico City. Then in 1860 the French arrived to make preparation for the future reign of Maximilian, whom they installed as Emperor, and his wife Carlota.

Veracruz is rich in folklore. The colorful costumes, dances and lively rhythms of the Veracruz musicians are among the most stirring in Mexico. A major event is the Veracruz Carnival which takes place annually before Lent.

This is one of the most important industrial regions of Mexico. The north has large gas fields and the whole of the Gulf region is synonymous with oil. Oil drilling is Mexico's number one extractive industry. Almost all the oilfields are centered around the Gulf, from the Gulf of Sabinas in the north to the Tampico/Pozo Rica central area and Tabasco/Chiapas in the south. The recent discoveries of new oilfields in the area have played a decisive role in Mexico's economy and it has taken over from tourism as Mexico's number one industry.

Gastromic specialities: Seafood, oysters, crab, shrimp soup, *Sopa de mariscos* (seafood soup), *Huachinango à la Veracruzana* (red snapper with a tomato sauce, peppers and onions), *carne à la Tampiqueña* (roast meat, Tampico style).

Festivals and events: Feb or Mar (week before Lent), colorful carnival with dances, music, fireworks and parades, Veracruz (Veracruz); Mar 18, festival to commemorate expropriation of oil, Poza Rica (Veracruz); Mar 18, festival of San José, Córdoba (Veracruz); Apr 12, Tampico festival (Veracruz); end June, annual

tarpon fishing tournament, Tuxpan (Veracruz); Sep 1, fiesta of San Miguel Arcangel, Orizaba (Veracruz); Nov 3, fiesta of San Martín de Porres, Tampico (Veracruz); Dec 8, fiesta of la Purísima Concepción, Córdoba (Veracruz). In this ever-changing country it is wise to check details of dates and times of events with the Mexican Tourist Office.

Catemaco N6
Veracruz (pop. 18,000). Lake Catemaco, near the town of the same name is worth visiting. It is believed to have been formed as a result of the eruption of seven volcanoes. The lake is surrounded by lovely scenery situated between two mountains with green hills sloping down to the lakeside. There is a thriving fishing industry based on the lake's abundance of trout, perch and the small white fish called *pepesca*. Water skiing and boat trips on the lake are available and there are some interesting Olmec ruins at **Hueyapán,** which is about 25 miles (40 km) south. *Mexico City 357 mi/575 km.*

Ciudad Victoria H1
Tamaulipas (pop. 180,000). Capital of Tamaulipas, Ciudad Victoria was named after the first President of Mexico, Guadalupe Victoria. The town has no particular tourist attractions but for those traveling south from the United States border it is a convenient place to stop, and it is an excellent center for sports, with a large football stadium, a bullring and good opportunities for hunting and fishing. You can make an interesting excursion to the nearby waterfall of **Juan Capitán.** *Mexico City 436 mi/702 km.*

Coatzacoalcos O6
Veracruz (pop. 110,000). Coatzacoalcos is an important industrial center and an oil and sulphur boom town. A railroad is under development which will link Coatzacoalcos with the Pacific port of Salina Cruz across the Isthmus of Tehuantepec. *Mexico City 464 mi/746 km.*

Córdoba N4
Veracruz (pop. 120,000). Córdoba is a pleasant little town with houses which are of pink and blue with red tiled roofs. The name can be derived from the Arabic *karba tuba* which means 'important city' and from the Spanish Viceroy Fernández de Córdoba who was responsible for designating the town as a city in 1618. Independence from the Spanish was finally won here and you can visit the Hotel Zevallos where the Independence Treaty of Córdoba was signed in 1821. Córdoba is the center of the coffee industry and is surrounded by coffee plantations. *Mexico City 183 mi/294 km.*

Fortín de las Flores N4
Veracruz (pop. 20,000). This town is well worth a stop. The Spanish meaning of Fortín de las Flores is 'Fortress of the Flowers' and it aptly describes this delightful little town which abounds in all varieties of flowers from gardenias and orchids to azaleas, bougainvilles and many more. The landscape is crowned by the snowy peak of Mexico's highest volcano — Pico de Orizaba. There are sugar, coffee and citrus plantations nearby and the warm, moist climate also accounts for the luxurious, tropical vegetation of this fertile region. *Mexico City 180 mi/290 km.*

Jalapa M4
Veracruz (pop. 250,000). Jalapa, which can also be spelled Xalapa, is the capital of the state of Veracruz. The town has a rich

Royal Ponsettia. Plants and flowers are an important feature of Fortín de las Flores

Dancers at Papantla

profusion of brilliantly-colored tropical flowers of many varieties. It has become an important cultural center with regular performances of ballet and modern dance. At the regional University, there is an excellent museum with important archaological pieces, displayed both indoors and outdoors from the Olmec, Totonac, Huastec and Aztec cultures. Jalapa can suffer from frequent bouts of fine drizzle, known locally as the *chipichipi*. Clouds from the Gulf build up over the town and it is often misty. Jalapa was built on seven hills and you can take a trip to the top of the highest of these, called Macuiltepec, from where there is a fine view of the Gulf when the weather is clear. *Mexico City 196 mi/ 315 km.*

Matamoros F3

Tamaulipas (pop. 300,000). Matamoros is a border town and a major port of entry to Mexico for those traveling from Texas. The town, which was founded in 1765, has had a turbulent past and was burned and ransacked several times during various conflicts in Mexico's history. It grew in prosperity during the United States Civil War when business was built up handling contraband goods for the Confederates. Matamoros is now an important industrial center for clothing, electronic and chemical goods and is the major producer of cotton in Mexico. Together with Tampico and Veracruz, Matamoros forms part of an important Gulf group of international commerce.

The town has a lively, pleasant zócalo, tree-lined paths with many impressive statues dedicated to the heroes of the past and a lovely park with a bandstand and much activity. Shopping facilities are good and the Arts and Crafts Center near the International Bridge contains many attractive Mexican handicrafts. *Mexico City 623 mi/1003 km.*

Nuevo Laredo C1

Tamaulipas (pop. 260,000). Border town and an important gateway from Texas to Mexico City. It is situated on the flat plains which characterize northern Mexico and its major industry is tourism. Thousands of visitors come to the town every year for its shopping, its numerous hotels, restaurants, lively nightlife, bullfights, dog and horse racing. The handicraft museum, which is in the downtown area has an attractive collection of Mexican arts and crafts. *Mexico City 733 mi/1180 km.*

Orizaba N3

Veracruz (pop. 150,000). Orizaba marks the halfway point between the plateau and the tropical coastlands. The vegetation in the town which comes from both regions reflects this. Orizaba is situated in magnificent country and the town is overlooked by the beautiful lofty snow-capped peak of the Pico de Orizaba volcano (also referred as Citlaltépetl which means morning star). Orizaba has a pleasant climate and an abundance of flowers. It is a great Mexican beer center and produces one of the country's finest beers, *Cervecería Montezuma*. Visits can be arranged to the brewery. A trip can be made to the lovely **Tuxpango Falls** in the area. *Mexico City 172 mi/ 276 km*

Papantla L3

Veracruz (pop. 125,000). Papantla is the center of Mexico's vanilla industry. It lies in a valley surrounded by vanilla orchid jungles and the area is fragrant with their aroma. This is the home of the *Voladores de Papantla*, the Flying Men of Papantla from the Totonac Indian civilization. This flying pole ceremony is most spectacular. It originally took place prior to Corpus Christi Day but is now performed most Sundays in the main square, weather permitting. Four dancers dressed in splendid costumes climb up to the top of a tall pole and, while a fifth performer on a tiny platform palys a haunting melody on the flute, the dancers twirl around the pole and down to the ground by means of a rope which unwinds, leaving them free to 'fly' around the pole in circles with arms extended. All four fly round 13 times, representing the four 13-year epochs which made up the 52-year life cycle of the ancient Totonacs. The local people are Totonac descendants and still wear beautiful, colorful costumes in their daily lives and for special festivities. The Totonacs, who earn quite a good living from the vanilla industry, are Mexico's only recognized polygamous tribe and it is quite common for some of the more affluent men to have several wives.

Their sacred city, **El Tajín** which is only partially restored, lies about 8 miles (13 km) from Papantla. The outstanding Pyramid of the Niches, which is seven stories high, was built with probably 365 niches decorating the whole building. The carvings on the Ball Court walls are also very interesting.

Another great Totonac city is to be found at **Zempoala**. There are several interesting pyramids and temples such as the Temple of the Small Faces which is worth examining for its skull carvings. *Mexico City 188 mi/303 km.*

Tampico J3

Tamaulipas (pop. 255,000). Tampico, which is the largest city in the state, was built near the mouth of the Pánuco river and is a major port serving the Gulf of Mexico. This thriving industrial town is an important oil refining center.

This was originally the site of an old Huastec settlement but it was destroyed by Cortés and his men who founded the early Tampico here in 1533. Early constructions were destroyed by hurricanes and floods and, as a result, buildings in present-day Tampico date back no further than the end of the 19th century. The hurricane season occurs during the winter and heavy rains can be expected during the hot humid months of summer.

There is a lot of activity around the port during the day and also a lively nightlife. The numerous bars and restaurants serve excellent fresh seafood. Crabs, known as *jaibas*, are among the freshest and tastiest in Mexico. The Plaza de Armas, which is the town's main square, is the social center with its many trees, birds, squirrels and a Moorish-style bandstand. On the north side of the square, you can see the cathedral which was built in 1931, thanks to the donations received from a Californian oil tycoon.

Playa Miramar beach is only a few minutes drive northeast of Tampico and the beach areas have some limited accommodations available. There are good opportunities for hunting and fishing. Several nearby freshwater lagoons, particularly **Laguna del Chariel** and **Laguna del Carpintero**, are worth visiting if you are an angler and there is deep-sea fishing in the Gulf. *Mexico City 291 mi/468 km.*

Tuxpan K3

Veracruz (pop. 60,000). Tuxpan (can also be spelled 'Tuxpam') is a sleepy fishing town built on the bank of the Tuxpan river. As is common in most Mexican towns and villages in Mexico, life revolves around the main plaza. Tuxpan is a fisherman's paradise and the annual Tuxpan fishing tournament, which takes place at the end of June, is a big attraction. You can make excursions northeast to the wild but attractive **Tamiahua Lagoon** and to the **Isla de Lobos** (Wolf Island), about 40 miles (64 km) away which is magnificent for skin diving *Mexico City 211 mi/340 km.*

Veracruz N5

Veracruz (pop. 305,000). Veracruz — which means the True Cross — is Mexico's major port and an important commercial center. The city has a strong Afro-Caribbean influence, noticeable in the style of architecture, the music and the people. For about a hundred years during the 16th and 17th centuries, African slaves were imported here and used as labor in the sugarcane and rice fields of the area. They have inter-married with people of Indian and Spanish origin over the years. Traces of today's Veracruzano's ancestry are still very much in evidence.

Veracruz has been the scene of a number of highly significant events in Mexico's history. The Conquistadores first landed here on Good Friday 1519, and founded the city. They planted a cross and named the area La Villa Rica de la Vera Cruz (the Rich Village of the True Cross) before setting forth on their march to the eventual conquest of Mexico. From the 16th to the 18th century Veracruz served as a trading port between Mexico and the Old World and the town was sacked and plundered several times by pirates who roamed the seas. At the end of the War of Independence, the Spaniard's last stronghold was the Castle of San Juan de Ulúa, across the bay, from where they bombarded the town. Veracruz has come under attack on several occasions when the French and Americans at different times sought to invade and occupy Mexico.

Structurally, the town's architecture shows a Spanish influence with buildings and overhanging balconies of stucco or wood, painted in more 'Caribbean' shades of pale pink, soft ochre and blue.

Street life in Veracruz is very lively and centers on the zócalo (known as Plaza de Armas or Plaza de la Constitución) which is surrounded by arcades and sidewalk cafés. You can while away a very pleasant few hours here drinking and sampling the delicious seafood while you are serenaded by the Veracruzano musicians who play lively rhythms on the guitar and delightful soft marimba music. On most evenings, while the area is busy with locals having their evening stroll or *paseo*, there are bandstand concerts.

Places of interest include la Parroquia church which overlooks the main square and the pleasant *malecón* (waterfront) from which you can take a boat to the **Isla de Sacrificios** (Island of Sacrifices). There is a good view of Veracruz from here and a small shrine where human sacrifices were once performed. The **Castle of San Juan de Ulúa** also stands in the bay on a small island. It was originally built here to defend the city but it was later used as a particularly disagreeable prison. It is now used as a convention center and is well worth a visit.

You can make a pleasant excursion to the little resort town of **Mocambo** which lies about 3 miles (5 km) to the south and has the best beach in the area with good swimming facilities. Beyond this lies the lovely exotic jungle lagoon of **Mandinga** in the middle of nowhere where you can take a boat trip through mangroves and eat delicious seafood at the lakeside restaurant.

One of Veracruz's biggest attractions is the Carnival which takes place just before Lent, with dancing, music and fireworks. *Mexico City 265 mi/427 km.*

Villahermosa O8

Tabasco (pop. 220,000). Although its name in Spanish means 'beautiful town', Villahermosa does little to justify such a description. Villahermosa is a boom town, right in the heart of oil country. The city seems more concerned with material prosperity than with charm. You may find that in some restaurants and bars, visitors, and particularly women, can feel somewhat out of place but the construction of a pedestrian shopping mall in the downtown area has made the center more attractive for tourists.

The city has two major attractions. La Venta museum, on the outskirts of town, has a magnificent outdoor display of archaeological exhibits from the Olmec culture. Here, in the exotic setting of a jungle park, you can marvel at the monolithic Olmec heads and sculptures, thought to date back some 3000 years. The pieces were brought to Villahermosa from the surrounding area when the oilfield developments began and are displayed in an environment similar to their natural setting. In the downtown area, the Tabasco Museum of Archaeology has a wonderful collection of sculptures and artifacts from the Olmec, Mayan and Toltec civilizations and full-scale reproductions of the famous Bonampak murals.

A drive of about 30 miles (48 km) to the south will lead you to the **Cocona Caves** which are worth visiting for their striking rock formations. Villahermosa plays a significant rôle in Mexico's tourist industry by serving as a gateway to the magnificent Mayan ruins at **Palenque** which lie about an hour and a half southeast of Villahermosa by road. As accommodations in the vicinity of the ruins are limited, tourists usually stay overnight in Villahermosa which has a selection of more comfortable hotels. You can take the local bus to Palenque, hire a car or take a tour. For more information on Palenque, which is situated in the neighboring state of Chiapas, see Southern Mexico. *Mexico City 535 mi/860 km.*

Dancers are always popular in Mexico

Villahermosa at night

The Gulf Region

Mexican girl ready for her part in the local fiesta

INDEX

All main entries are printed in heavy type. Map references are also printed in heavy type.
The map page number precedes the grid reference.

Acapulco **50-1 E5**, 51-3	Camping 22	Cuicuilco (pyramids) 46
Accidents, road 18	**Cancún** **64 B10**, 65	**Culiacán** **104-5 K11**, 104
Accommodations 18-19	Car ferries 15-16	**Currency** 13-14
apartments/condominiums 19	Car insurance 17	**Customs** 13
camping 22	Carmen Convent 47	for all visitors 13
hotels 18-19	Carrizalejo (springs) 104	for Canadians 13
reservations 19	Casas Grandes 111	for U.K. citizens 13
Acolman, convent of 47,93	Cascabeles, Lake 104	for U.S. residents 13
Addresses, useful 31	Cascada de Basaseáchic 111	Cuyutlán 81
Adolfo López Mateos	**Catemaco** **118 N6**, 119	
reservoir 104	Caves of the Sleeping Sharks 71	Dainzu 57
Aguascalientes **110 N8**, 109	Ceboruco lava fields 108	Dentists 28
Air services 14, 15	Cenote Sagrado 70	Desierto de los Leones 95
internal 15	**Central Mexico** 85-95, **86**	Discotheques 26
to Mexico 14-15	festivals and events 86-7	Doctors 28
Ajijic **75 E4**, 77	Centro Artesanal Buenavista 47	emergency phone numbers 28
Alameda Park 44	Chancanab lagoon 71	**Dolores Hidalgo** **86 B3**, 88
Álamos **104-5 H9**, 103-4	**Chapala** **75 E5**, 77	Drinks see Food and drink
Almoloya 95	Chapultepec Park 42, 45, 88	**Driving** 15, 17-18
Animals, importation of 13	Charreadas (rodeo) 22	accidents 18
Antiquities, exportation of 28	Chetumal **64 G8**, 67	automobile organization 31
Apartments see Accommodations	**Chiapa de Corzo**	breakdown 18
Architecture 11	**50-1 E18**, 53	car rental 18
Arenitas (springs) 104	**Chichén Itzá** **64 C7**, 69-70	highway conditions 17
Arts, the 10-11	ground plan 68	insurance 17
architecture 11	Chicomoztoc (ruins) 112	license 17
early civilizations 10-11	**Chihuahua** **110 F4**, 109-111	parking 18
literature 11	**Chilpancingo** **50-1 D6**, 53	police 18
painting 11	Chinipaque Mesa 115	precautions 17-18
post-conquest 11	Cholula 90	road safety 17
Automobile organization	Churches 28	useful words 18
(Mexican) 31	Cigarettes and tobacco 28	**Durango** **110 L6**, 112
Aztecs 8-9	Cinema 26	Duty-free allowances 13
	Ciudad Juárez **110 C3**, 111	Dzibilchaltún 72
Bacalar, Lake 67	Ciudad Universitaria 46	
Baja California 97-101, **98**	**Ciudad Victoria** **118 H1**, 119	Eating places see Food and
festivals and events 99	Climbing 25	drink
Baja Sur 99	**Coatzacoalcos** **118 O6**, 119	Edzná 65
Balancanché Cave 70	Coba 67	Electricity 28
Ballet 26	Cocona caves 123	El Cubilete 89
Banco Nacional de México 44	Cola de Caballo (falls) 115	El Farallón island 108
Banks 14	**Colima** **75 G4**, 77	El Garrafón 71
opening hours 29	**Comitán** **50-1 F19**, 53-4	El Salto (falls) 108
Barranca del Cobre	Concepción de Oro 112	El Tajin 121
(Copper Canyon) 106, 111	Condominiums see	Embassies see Consulates
Basílica de Guadalupe 42, 47	Accommodations	Emergency phone calls 28
Bataoto, Lake 104	Consulates (addresses) 31	**Ensenada** **98 D1**, 100
Bazar Sábado 46, 47	Contoy island 67, 71	**Entertainment** 25-6
Best buys 30	Copilco 46	Estadio Azteca 46
Bonampak 59	**Córdoba** **118 N4**, 121	Estadio J. Lopez P. 46
Bullfighting 22	Coronados island 101	Estadio Olimpico 46
Bus services 15, 16-17	Cortés Pass 90	Exchange facilities 14
from U.S.A. 15	**Cozumel** **64 D10**, 70-1	Excursions, organized 17
internal 16-17	Craft centers 47	
	Credit cards accepted 14	Ferries 15-16
Cabo San Lucas **98 O9**, 99	Cruising 15, 22	**Fiestas, national** 26-8
Cacahuamilpa (caves) 61, 88	**Cuautla** **86 G7**, 87	local see under regions
Calixtlahuaca 95	**Cuernavaca** **86 F6**, 87-8	Fishing:
Campeche **64 E4**, 65		fresh water 22

126

Index   127

sea	22
FONART stores	30
FONATUR	7, 65, 101
Food and drink	20-22
Fortín de las Flores	**118 N4**, 119
Frontón *see Jai alai*	
Fuel	18
Galería de Historia	45
Galleries *see Museums and galleries*	
García caves	113-15
Geography	6
Golf	22
Government	7
Guadalajara	**75 D5**, 77-80
town plan	78-9
Guadalupe	100
Guaymas	**104-5 G7**, 104
Guerrero Negro	**98 H4**, 100
Gulf region	117-23, **118**
festivals and events	117-19
Health	28
insurance	12-13, 28
Hermosillo	**104-5 F7**, 104
History	8-10
Horseback riding	22-4
Hospitals	28
emergency phone number	28
Hotels	18-19
rates	19
reservations	19
Huasteca canyon	115
Hunting	24
Hueyapán	119
Iguala	**50-1 B6**, 54
Imala (springs)	104
Information, general	28-34
Information in Mexico	28, 29
Insurance	12-13
car	17
health	12-13, 28
Irapuato	**86 C2**, 89
Isla Carmen	101
Isla de Lobos	122
Isla de Sacrificios	122
Isla Mujeres	**64 B10**, 71
Ixtapa	**50-1 C2**, 54
Ixtapán de la Sal	95
Jocotepec	**75 E4**, 80
Jai alai (frontón)	24, 48
Jalapa	**118 M4**, 119-21
Janitzio	82
Jarácuaro island	82
Juan Capitán (falls)	119
Kino Bay	**104-5 F6**, 106
Kohúnlich	67
La Bufadora	100
Laguna del Carpintero	122
Laguna del Chariel	122
Laguna Santa María	108
Lagunas de Montebello	54
Lambityeco	57
Language	31-4
useful expressions	34
La Pacanda	82
La Paz	**98 N8**, 100
Las Lomas	46
La Tobara (springs)	108
Lázaro Cárdenas	82
León	**86 B2**, 89
Literature	11
Loreto	**98 K7**, 100-101
Los Cocos beach	71
Los Mochis	**104-5 J9**, 106
Lost property	28
Macurimi (springs)	104
Magazines	29
Mail	28-9
Central Post Office	31
Malinalco	88
Manzanillo	**75 G3**, 80-1
Mariquita, Lake	104
Matamoros	**118 F3**, 121
Mazatlán	**104-5 M12**, 106-8
Medical treatment	28
Mérida	**64 C5**, 72
Metepec	95
Mexcaltitlán	**104-5 N13**, 108
Mexicali	**98 C3**, 101
Mexico City	35-48, **36-40**
downtown	42-5
entertainment	48
festivals and events	48
markets	47
southern Mexico City	46-7
Sundays in	47-8
transport	41-2
Zona Rosa	45-6
Misión de Santa Rosalía	101
Mismaloya beach	82
Mitla	55
Mocambo	122
Monclova	**110 H9**, 112
Monte Albán	57
ground plan	56
Monterrey	**114 C5**, 113
Morelia	**75 F9**, 81
Mulegé	**98 J6**, 101
Museums and galleries:	
Antropología	45
Arte Moderno	45
Arte Popular	44
Ciudad de México	44
Culturas	44
Frida Kahlo	47
Galería de Historia	45
National Arts	44
Opening hours	29
Rufino Tamayo	45
Music	25-6
Newspapers	29
Nichupte Lagoon	66-7
Nightclubs	26
Nogales	**104-5 C7**, 108
North, the	109-12, **110**
festivals and events	109
Northeast, the	113-15, **114**
festivals and events	113
Northwest, the	103-8, **104-5**
festivals and events	103
Nuevo Laredo	**118 C1**, 121
Oaxaca	**50-1 D11**, 54
Oaxtepec	87
Ocotlán	55
Old San Blas	108
Opening times	29
Opera	26
Orizaba	**118 N3**, 121
Pachuca	**86 D7**, 89
Painting	11
Palancar Reef	70-1
Palenque	**50-1 D19**, 59
ground plan	58
Panteón (Guanajuato)	89
Papantla	**118 L3**, 121
Paperwork	12-13
Paracho	84
Parking	18
Passports	12
Pátzcuaro	**75 F8**, 81-2
lake	82
Pedregal	47
Pharmacies	28
Photography	29
Pie de la Cuesta	53
Playa Azul	**75 I6**, 82
Playa las Gatas	61
Playa Miramar beach	122
Police	18, 29
Population (Mexico)	6
Postal services *see Mail*	
Progreso	**64 B5**, 72
Public holidays	29
Puebla	**86 F8**, 89-90
Puerto Angel	**50-1 G11**, 59
Puerto Escondido	**50-1 G10**, 59
Puerto Vallarta	**75 D1**, 82-4
Querétaro	**86 C4**, 91
Rabies	13
Rail services	15, 16
Restaurants *see also Food and drink*	21
Road safety/conditions	17
Rosarito	**98 H4**, 101
Sailing *see also Cruising*	24
Saltillo	**110 J9**, 112
San Ángel	46-7
San Benito	100
San Blas	**104-5 O14**, 108
San Cristóbal de las Casas	

Index

	50-1 E18, 59	Tecuén	82
Sanctuario de Atotonilco	91	Tehuacán	90
San Felipe	**98 E3**, 101	**Tehuantepec**	**50-1 F13**, 61
San Francisco beach	71	Telegrams	30, 31
San Francisco, Church of	44	Telephones	30
San José del Cabo	**98 O9**, 101	useful numbers	31
San Juan del Rio	**86 D5**, 91	Tennis	25
San Juan de Ulúa castle	122	Templo Mayor	44
San Lorenzo, Lake	104	Tenancingo	95
San Luis Potosí	**114 H4**, 115	Tenayuca	95
San Miguel	71	Teopanzolco	88
San Miguel de Allende		**Teotihuacán**	**86 E7**, 93
	86 C3, 91	ground plan	92
Santa Ana	95	**Tepic**	**104-5 O14**, 108
Santa Cecilia	95	**Topolobampo**	**104-5 J9**, 108
Santa Clara del Cobra	84	**Tepotzotlán**	**86 E6**, 94
Santa Maria del Río	115	church	47
Santa Maria hills	81	Tepoztlán	88
Santa Rosalía	**98 J6**, 101	Tequesquitengo, Lake	88
Scammons lagoon	100	**Tequila**	**75 D4**, 84
Scuba and skin diving	24	Theater	26
Sea services	15-16	Tianguistengo	95
Shopping	29-30	Tiburón	106
best buys	30	Time differentials	30
FONART stores	30	Tipping	30-1
markets	29, 47	Tlacolula	55
opening times	29	Tlaquepaque	80
Sierra de Tarahumara	111	**Tlaxcala**	**86 E8**, 95
Siqueiros Polyforum	46	Toilets	31
Soccer	24	**Toluca**	**86 F6**, 95
South, the	49-62, **50-1**	Tonala	80
festivals and events	51	**Torreón**	**110 J7**, 112
Spas	24	Tourist card	12
Speed limits	17	Tourist offices	31
Sumódero Canyon	53	Trains *see* Rail services	
Sunbathing	25	Transport in Mexico City	41-2
Surfing	24-5	**Travel information**	14-17
Swimming	25	internal	15-17
		length of stay allowed	12
Tamiahua lagoon	122	package tours	15
Tampico	**118 L3**, 121-2	to Mexico	14-15
Tapachula	**50-1 I9**, 59-60	Travel documents	12-13
Taxco	**50-1 B5**, 60-1	for all visitors	12
Taxis	17		
Tecate	**98 C1**, 101		

for Canadians	12		
for U.K. citizens	12		
for U.S. citizens	12		
insurance	12-13		
Tula	**86 D6**, 95		
Tule tree	55		
Tulum	67		
Tuxpan	**118 K3**, 122		
Tuxpango falls	121		
Tuxtla Guitiérrez			
	50-1 E7, 61		
Tzaráracua (falls)	84		
Uruápan	**75 G7**, 84		
Uxmal	**64 D5**, 74		
ground plan	70		
Valenciana, church of la	89		
Valladolid	**64 C8**, 74		
Valle de Bravo	**86 F4**, 95		
Veracruz	**118 N5**, 122-3		
Vigia (springs)	104		
Villahermosa	**118 O8**, 123		
Walking	25		
Water skiing	25		
West, the	75-84, **75**		
festivals and events	76-7		
Windsurfing	25		
Xcaret	67		
Xel-Ha	67		
Xochicalco	88		
Xochimilco floating gardens			
	42, 46		
Yagul	57		
Yaxchilán	59		
Yelapa	84		
Yucatán Peninsula	63-74, **64**		
Yunuén	82		
Zacatecas	**110 M8**, 112		
Zempoala	121		
Zihuatanejo	**50-1 C2**, 61		